Wilbur Moore

THE CARR GUIDE TO PERSONAL WEALTH

DEENA MARIE CARR

THE CARR GUIDE TO PERSONAL WEALTH

ISBN: 978-0-9846515-2-8

Published by

LIFEBRIDGE
BOOKS

P.O. Box 49428
Charlotte, NC 28277

Printed in the United States of America.

Dedication

I dedicate this book to my Mom. Without your prayers, motivation, and support, this book and so many other efforts would still be "ideas."

Contents

INTRODUCTION

In my first book, *Wealth, Grow it God's Way,* we discussed how to understand and align our mindset with a biblical mindset on wealth. I have been encouraged by those who have written or told me personally how the book helped them think about faith and finances totally differently. They were excited to see a new way of looking at money and wealth.

In this book, *A Guide to Personal Wealth,* my purpose is to establish a comprehensive framework that allows us to systematically build and manage money.

It is clear that we are living in very challenging times of great change—some of the most momentous for the U.S. and globally. In the midst of this, however, there is significant opportunity for great financial success, but there is also the risk of devastating financial collapse.

While everyone prefers *great success* to failure, many would be quite content financially with something more simple like "solid and consistent performance that avoids **investment sinkholes** (i.e., ...sudden and dramatic losses of wealth which crushes us financially with little warning)." But, even the most reasonable of performance expectations these days are fraught with questions, such as:

- So what is the most effective way to create wealth when there are a myriad of options?
- How do I ensure that I can preserve and increase wealth in these difficult times?
- How do I effectively manage this wealth on a daily basis?
- As I work on increasing wealth, how do I ensure that I am remaining focused on building the kingdom of God and not building barns for myself?

These questions and many others bombard us—and sometimes even overwhelm us—as we try to process the massive amount of financial information that we are fed on a daily basis.

In the upcoming chapters, I am going to discuss and explore a framework which I call the *Goshen Wealth Management Framework (GoWeM)* ©. This provides believers with a comprehensive approach for managing wealth or beginning to grow your portfolio.

Why do we call it the *Goshen Wealth Management Framework*? Let's look at Genesis. In Chapter 45, we see one of the most poignant passages in the Bible.

This is when Joseph reveals to his brothers that he is there lost sibling, Joseph.

> *And Joseph said to his brothers, "Please come near to me." So they came near. Then he said: "I am Joseph your brother, whom you sold into Egypt. But now, do not therefore be grieved or angry with yourselves because you sold me here; for God sent me before you to preserve life. For these two years the famine has been in the land, and there are still five years in which there will be neither plowing nor harvesting. And God sent me before you to preserve a posterity for you in the earth, and to save your lives by a great deliverance. So now it was not you who sent me here, but God; and He has made me a father to Pharaoh, and lord of all his house, and a ruler throughout all the land of Egypt. "Hurry and go up to my father, and say to him, 'Thus says your son Joseph: "God has made me lord of all Egypt; come down to me, do not tarry. You shall dwell in the land of Goshen, and you shall be near to me, you and your children, your children's children, your flocks and your herds, and all that you have. There I will provide for you, lest you and your household, and all that you have,*

come to poverty; for there are still five years of famine."' (verses 4-11).

A closer look shows us that the unimaginably difficult circumstances of Joseph's life journey was for a purpose. It was to make sure that Abraham's seed made it to Goshen and received the provision that God had provided for them. Let's read verses 10-12 again:

> *You shall dwell in the land of Goshen, and you shall be near to me, you and your children, your children's children, your flocks and your herds, and all that you have. There I will provide for you, lest you and your household, and all that you have, come to poverty; for there are still five years of famine.*

There had already been two years of famine, and there were still five more years of drought to go, but God had already prepared Goshen and all of its abundance to preserve His people.

Recently in the U.S. and throughout the globe, we have seen very challenging times financially. And while in some ways it has gotten better or at least, not yet gotten worse, it is clear that there are very uncertain days ahead. I believe it now more than ever, that we the people of God must really be "wise" and "divinely guided" in every area of our lives, especially in finances.

There is much work to be done and God will bless us richly in completing His work, if we are following Him. Yes, there is turmoil on the horizon. In the case of Joseph, the time of famine was not completely over, so it is essential for us to hear God's direction on how to *"go to and abide in Goshen"* during these difficult days.

The Goshen Framework builds upon the notion of the "seed." The seed is a powerful and popular concept in the Bible. It traditionally refers to a number of things including:

- The harvest of grain, fruit, etc.
- Lineage or children
- The Word of God
- The Kingdom of Heaven
- Faith

The "seed" also refers to money or resources, which we see in 2 Corinthians 9: 8-11:

And God is able to make all grace abound toward you, that you, always having all sufficiency in all things, may have an abundance for

> *every good work. As it is written: "He has dispersed abroad, He has given to the poor; His righteousness endures forever." Now may He* ***who supplies seed to the sower****, and bread for food, supply and* ***multiply the seed you have sown and increase the fruits of your righteousness****, while you are enriched in everything for all liberality, which causes thanksgiving through us to God.*

This is why when people teach, preach, or write about money and the Bible, they often refer to this concept of "the seed."

In the *Goshen Wealth Management Framework©*, we are going to take this concept of the seed even further to develop a comprehensive way of looking at a number of things from creating an income to understanding the economy, from investing to eliminating debt.

The Framework is also a foundational tool for sorting through the morass of information and misinformation that exists, to put together a comprehensive approach for managing our financial lives according to the principles of the Word of God.

Financial security comes as a result of a process that is always grounded first and foremost in God. We do not have to wait for "luck" or a "winning lottery ticket." The Creator has placed in His children the ability to access His abundance.

Over the past twenty years, my work with major financial institutions has reaffirmed my belief that faith and finances work hand in hand. It has affirmed for me that God is the creator of all things, including wealth. *He is not broke, and we shouldn't be either.*

Chapter 1

The Spiritual Context of Building and Managing Wealth

Wealth does not begin in the natural; it begins in the spiritual. This is because wealth ultimately comes from and belongs to God.

– Deena Marie Carr, Wealth, Grow it God's Way

There has been much written and preached about concerning the Bible, wealth, and prosperity. Even in *Wealth, Grow it God's Way*, we not only took time to define wealth and explore its purpose in the life of the believer, but we also looked at the types of riches discussed in the Bible and God's instruction to His children regarding how He *"has given them the power to get wealth"*—and what we then are supposed to do regarding our finances.

We rightly concluded with the fact that wealth begins in the spiritual realm because it ultimately comes from God.

If we are to become effective builders and managers of wealth, *we have to take this understanding to the next level.*

If you look at the story of creation in Genesis, we see that on each day, God finished a different part of His work. On the seventh day, the Bible states that God rested from *"all that He had created."* So my question to you is, "Does Genesis have an "eighth day"? After the Sabbath, is there another day in which God continues with one more round of creating?"

The answer is "no." There is no eighth day.

Why do we begin the discussion of the Goshen Wealth Management Framework with this point? In building and managing wealth, why is it significant that there is no eighth day of creation? It is because of this very important fact:

> *Everything that God is going to create, He has already created.*
>
> – Pastor Mary T. Carr

My Pastor stated this several years ago during a sermon, and as I began to really reflect and ponder this from a financial perspective, I realized that up to that moment, I had been glossing over a really important element in my understanding and teaching about wealth and money. A point that was so nuanced, but yet so critical in aligning and fine tuning our understanding of money, the pursuit of wealth, and "kingdom stewardship." If we get this wrong, it throws off everything that we do financially. What do I mean by this? Let's take a closer look.

Many people now understand that God is their source. They know they need to put the Lord first in their financial lives and their financial endeavors. They even demonstrate this by faithfully paying their tithes, giving offerings and prioritizing several other charitable causes. People also understand that as they are successful in obtaining finances, it was God who had not only blessed them with the wealth, but had given them the power to obtain it.

So if all of this and more is true, why is it that

believers are still so stressed about money? Why are they so worried over their investment portfolios or lack thereof? Why are they anxious whether their "401k has become a 101k?"

Why did the recent global economic crisis shake our financial core and cause so many of us to fret about our future and whether or not we had the appropriate levels of wealth to keep ourselves in the lifestyle to which we and our family had become accustomed? There are probably numerous reasons, but there is one in particular that I would like to focus on now.

THE SOURCE OF WEALTH

I believe that a key factor regarding why we can become so stressed and fearful about wealth is because we actual believe that **we** are the ones who must **create that wealth**. After all, "God helps those who helps themselves."

We convince ourselves that it is by the sweat of our brow in our physical work efforts that allows us to create the resources we need. After all, doesn't 2 Thessalonians 3:10 tell us that if we don't work, we don't eat? In fact, isn't it Genesis 3:17 which tells us that the price of Adam's disobedience was that he was going to have to work by the sweat of his brow?

Yes, we believe that it is our intellect, our study, and our "witty inventions" which allow us to come up with the ideas that **make** us money and **make** us rich. This is why we work so hard in our careers to put in the long hours, to endear ourselves to the right people, so that we are promoted to our desired level. It is why we get so upset when the doors are closed or the promotions/raises do not come through.

Believing that **we** are the creators of wealth is why so many of us have given our lives to the businesses that we have built because **they *create*** income and wealth, not only for ourselves, but also for family, friends, and numerous other people in the company and the entire supply chain.

On a spiritual level, we even believe that it is our work at being a good Christian that positions us to receive God's blessings and favor, and thus bring to ourselves more income and more wealth.

In all of this, **we are at the center of what I will call the <u>wealth creation process</u>**. After all, isn't that what is meant by Deuteronomy 8:18 when it says that God has given ***us the power*** to obtain wealth?

There is a reason (probably several) why Proverbs 23:4 tells us not to exhaust ourselves trying to get rich. But expending our energies trying to *be* wealthy, trying to *stay* wealthy, or worrying that we are not wealthy, is exactly what too many of us have done. And I believe that it is a trick of the enemy to distract and wear out God's children.

You see, when we reflect on the first chapters of Genesis, there is a critical understanding that we must tap into and allow to direct and guide our lives, which is this: If God has created everything that He is going to create, and, if *"there is nothing new under the sun,"* according to Ecclesiastes; **then, we do not and actually cannot "create" wealth because wealth has already been created.**

Goshen Principle #1: We do not create wealth. We tap into the wealth that God has already created for us.

An often quoted scripture is Jeremiah 1:5: *"Before I formed you in the womb I knew you, before you were born I set you apart."*

This verse shows that God not only has a purpose and a destiny for all of us before we were ever born, but, it also lets us know that God, being the loving Father He is, has already provided for us. And like a good Father, He provides abundantly for His children.

So let's take this one step further and look at a woman who we will call Denise, and say that God has already appointed maximum provision for her. It was established before she was born that she could have a $100 million dollar clothing company designing clothes, which she loves to do.

How does Denise tap into this $100 million dollar purpose and destiny? Surely she will need to prepare herself by doing things such as learning about clothing design, running an enterprise, choosing the right business partners, etc. And yes, she will need to be a smart, committed worker and leader.

But Denise could spend a lifetime, working herself to the bone, and never have $100,000 let alone $100 million. It is going to take a lot of listening to God to understand the path, steps, and turns along the way that He has mapped out for her to reach the $100 million goal.

On the other hand, Denise could time everything perfectly and build the $100 million dollar business and be lauded on the cover of every trade magazine for her success. Yet, she could lose it all in a moment, because she did not slow down enough to hear God when He was telling her that now was the time to (or not to) make a bold new strategic move.

Goshen Principle #2: The key to wealth is obedience to God, not obsession about work or accumulation.

When we realize and focus more on "tapping into wealth" than on the prideful position of being masters of our own destiny and creators of our own universe—for which we will give God a portion as thanks—we shift the entire energy and focus of our lives. The goal is not about the exchange of work for money or exchange of great strategies for wealth. Instead, the path to true riches for the believer is obedience to God on a moment by moment basis in everything we do and every decision that we make.

The Work-Life Balance

One of the ways that can be a clear sign that we are absorbed with creating our own wealth instead of tapping into the wealth that God has already created for us is by looking at our allocation of time.

I am struck by the fact that in large and small churches alike, there are many people in the house of God on Sundays, but when it comes to weekday Bible studies, prayer sessions, and other activities, there is only a small fraction of the congregation in attendance. The most common reason is almost always related directly or indirectly to work. I know first hand because I have been guilty.

Work requires many of us to spend long hours on the job, which often does not allow time during the week for too much else. This is especially true during a financial crisis, as companies try to increase profits and strengthen their balance sheets. They ask fewer and fewer employees to work longer and harder. The reward for many has not been a pay raise, but the simple gratitude of keeping their jobs.

For those who have a few moments after work, by the time they pick up their children, help them with their homework or prepare dinner for the spouse and complete a few chores, there is hardly a minute extra to spare or enough energy to make it to the church during the week. For others, it is the commitment to get your "temple" in better shape, so the choice of going to the church during weekdays gets in the way of workouts and other social activities.

All of this makes sense if we are the creators of our wealth.

On Sunday, or whatever day you choose, you go to church and fellowship with other believers. The rest of the week you are about the business of creating wealth. When you have finished this objective, or when you reach the point where you have so much money you have unlimited free time, then you will spend more time at church. But, right now, we rationalize that God has to understand we are trying to "make a better life for ourselves and our family."

We think that God would surely understand that the only reason we are not spending more time with Him is that we are working on leaving *"an inheritance to our children's children"* (Proverbs 13:22).

This pattern of behavior not only applies to making it to midweek prayer or Bible study, but to how much personal time and devotion we spend with God. Sometimes, we are working so hard that all we have time for is to wake up and run out the door or jump on the computer and work, work, work on the treadmill of life until we drop.

We have pocket Bibles and various translations on our computers, smart phones, and tablet PC's, yet we are still unable to slow down enough to quietly read and meditate on the Word. This is a clear red flag.

Yes, I believe we can go through *a season* in our lives where we have to put in longer hours because we are on a special project or we are temporarily at a particular level in the organization where we may have to prove ourselves or work through challenges. However, if month after month and year after year passes, and we still have the excuse that work and the pursuit of money for the purpose of accumulation or even survival, keeps us from what we know to be the correct balance, then something is wrong—very wrong.

Goshen Principle #3: Pray about and carefully scrutinize situations in which the pursuit of wealth takes us away from the

quality time we spend alone with God, in fellowship with believers, and sharing the Gospel.

A word of caution:

Everywhere we go, the signs of the imminent return of the Messiah are all around us. And we know that the financial shaking that occurred with the recent global economic crisis is not over. If anything, there is far more to come in the days and years ahead. But Genesis 26 shows us that Isaac sowed in a time of famine and reaped a hundredfold blessing. He was so prosperous that he was envied by those of his day.

As a son of the covenant, Isaac knew to listen to the Lord for direction on how to prosper. If we read chapter 26 closely, we see that Isaac did not have increase because he worked harder than anyone else. **Isaac prospered because he obeyed God when He told him to go contrary to popular thought (which was to move to Egypt during the time of famine, which his children would later do) and instead "dwell in this land." Isaac listened.**

The shaking that is clearly on the horizon will require that we be spiritually attuned and not just financial astute. Now is the time to store up the wealth of prayer, Bible study, and consecration so that the "voice of a stranger" we will not hear. Even when the cries and chaos are deafening, we will be able to listen to the still, quiet voice of our Savior guiding us to safety. For after all, *"It is not by might or by power, but by the Spirit says the Lord"* (Zechariah 4:6).

Summary:

We understand that as children of God, we can expect His abundance and provision. However, always remember that godly wealth is something that **we tap into and it is not something that we create on our own.** We draw from His resources through obedience to God and by keeping Him first as the wealth is manifested.

The global economic crisis has thrown conventional wisdom and many of the pillars of economic theory on its side. To stay calm and make the right choices during this time requires prayer and godly wisdom, not just man's advice. This is why the first level of the *Goshen Wealth Management Framework* © begins with the understanding that everything is first and foremost happening on the **spiritual level**. If we miss the spiritual context of wealth, we can miss much, if not all, that God has appointed for us.

Practical Application

Today, sit down and assess your financial position

by looking at things such as:

- Income and income sources
- Total Assets
- Expenses
- Short and Long term liabilities (i.e., debt)

Also do an audit of your schedule. Look at your allocation of time and energy on a daily, weekly, monthly and yearly basis.

- If you create percentage allocations for your time, what would this look like?
- How have your time allocations changed over the years?
- How should you or how would you like to better allocate your time and energy?
- What do you expect them to be in the upcoming year? Will you be giving your best?
- Is this what God is asking from you right now?
- If you are in a season where your time is out of balance, how long do you expect it to last? How will you ensure that it will not continue?

If you are not doing so already, make it a habit to outline each action that you are going to take to build wealth (e.g., changing the investment allocation in your 401k, purchasing a stock, selling a piece of real estate, etc.).

Pray about each major action and listen for guidance and direction. This may sound very hokey or completely overly spiritualized. But I have found that all the degrees and training that I have in finance, economics, and analytics are not the only things needed to prosper. What is essential is for us to hear from the Lord, especially in times like these.

CHAPTER 2

ECONOMIC REALITIES

In the last chapter we talked about the Spiritual Context of wealth.

We began there because everything that we do as believers begins and ends in the Spirit. God is the Alpha and Omega, so He has the first and final say with everything in our lives, especially in our finances.

However, I do not want to leave you with the belief that all that is required to build wealth is to pray and trust God. Remember James 2:17 tells us that faith without works is dead.

Growing up, I saw plenty of people who trusted God unequivocally, but it did not mean that they had financial wealth. In fact, if I were to reflect over the last twenty-plus years of working with and speaking to individuals in the area of finances, I can say that I have continued to meet men and women who absolutely had "off the charts" faith in God, but in far too many cases, they were not fulfilling their potential financially.

Praying and trusting the Lord in all that we do is the "**given**." It is how we keep our covenant with Him. Now, we must add to our prayers and trust, **wisdom and understanding,** so the second layer of the Goshen Wealth Management Framework is The Economic Context.

Goshen Principle #4: In making financial decisions, we cannot completely ignore the economic environment. Wisdom requires that we understand both current and expected economic conditions.

Why the Economic Context? Isn't it much better to jump into a list of the "all time greatest investments"?

Or better still, shouldn't we explore the "ten greatest ways to decrease spending and eliminate debt" so that we have more to invest? The answer is "no."

Jumping to tactics without properly understanding the environment is putting the cart before the donkey. To explain why, let's go back to the seed metaphor that we talked about in the introduction.

Farmers don't just grab the best seed they can find and plant it. First, they spend a great deal of time and resources understanding current and future weather and soil conditions. These elements indicate a number of important things: the time to plant, the type of seeds that would be best to plant, the amount of additional water needed, required fertilizers, when the crop will be ready to harvest, the potential quality of the crop, and much more.

Our financial lives follow the same metaphor. In making decisions about our financial future and that of our family, it is important to step back and assess the short and long-term "weather" conditions.

Our decisions should take into account what we expect the economy to do or not do. It should also include alternative plans and strategies, in the event the "economic weather" is very different than we expect.

Some may say, *"Look, I am not operating in man's economy, I am on God's system. What goes on with this economy is inconsequential. In fact, between December 2007 and June 2009, when the U.S. was in the Great Recession—the longest and deepest recession in the last 70 years—God's Economy was just fine!"*

Yes, you are absolutely right. In fact, I agree wholeheartedly. But, I want to push you to think even more radically.

A CONTRARIAN STRATEGY?

One of the ways we can make sure that we operate in *God's economy* is to prayerfully understand what is going on with *man's system* and follow His leading in taking very different actions.

So what does this mean? Am I just suggesting the age-old "contrarian investment strategy?" Not really (but that would not be a bad start. Contrarian investing has worked very well for Warren Buffet). What I am highlighting here is that sometimes the way to really distinguish how God is leading you is by being aware of what conventional wisdom dictates at any given time.

Let's look at Gideon in Judges 7. Conventional wisdom was that if you were going to go to battle, clearly you should take as many soldiers with you as possible. Gideon was prepared with an army of over

30,000. But as Gideon moved forward, he heard the voice of the Lord telling him to take a different course, such as sending back the soldiers who were afraid or only taking those men who could drink water in a particular manner. In the end, Gideon was left with 300 warriors, but the army was victorious.

Will every "divinely guided" investment move sound as extreme as Gideon's actions? Probably not. Sometimes, God leads us to pay attention to economic signals that others are ignoring because of their excessive exuberance, excessive pessimism, or just plain ignorance. This is exactly what happened with the collapse of the U.S. housing market. There were clear indications that the real estate market was a bubble that was ready to burst before it actually did in 2007. Those who were paying attention either got out or stayed on the sidelines altogether.

There were even indications that the derivative securities which were faulted with causing the monumental collapse of the real estate market were going to wreak havoc on the economy. Below are edited excerpts that I found of Warren Buffet from his 2002 Berkshire Hathaway Annual Report.

I view derivatives as time bombs, *both for the parties that deal in them* **and the economic system.** *Basically these instruments call for money to change hands at some future date, with the amount to be determined by one or more reference* *items, such as interest rates, stock prices, or currency values. For example, if you are either long or short an S&P 500 futures contract, you are a party to a very simple derivatives transaction, with your gain or loss derived from movements in the index. Derivatives contracts are of varying duration, running sometimes to 20 or more years, and their value is often tied to several variables.*

Unless derivatives contracts are collateralized or guaranteed, their ultimate value also depends on the creditworthiness of the counter-parties to them. But before a contract is settled, the counter-parties record profits and losses—often huge in amount—in their current earnings statements without so much as a penny changing hands. Reported earnings on derivatives are often wildly overstated. That's because today's earnings are in a significant way based on estimates whose inaccuracy may not be exposed for many years.

The errors usually reflect the human tendency to take an optimistic view of one's commitments. But the parties to derivatives also have enormous incentives to cheat in accounting for them. Those who trade derivatives are usually paid, in whole or part, on "earnings" calculated by mark-to-market accounting. But often there is no real market, and "mark-to-model" is utilized. This substitution can bring on large-scale mischief. As a general rule, contracts involving multiple reference items and distant settlement dates increase the opportunities for counter-parties to use fanciful assumptions. The two parties to the contract might well use differing models allowing both to show substantial profits for many years. In extreme cases, mark-to-model degenerates into what I would call mark-to-myth.

I can assure you that the marking errors in the derivatives business have not been symmetrical. Almost invariably, they have favored either the trader who was eyeing a multi-million dollar bonus or the CEO who wanted to report impressive "earnings" (or both). The bonuses were paid, and the CEO profited from his options. Only much later did shareholders learn that the reported earnings were a sham.

Another problem about derivatives is that they can exacerbate trouble that a corporation has run into for completely unrelated reasons. This pile-on effect occurs because many derivatives contracts require that a company suffering a credit downgrade immediately supply collateral to counter-parties. Imagine then that a company is downgraded because of general adversity and that its derivatives instantly kick in with their requirement, imposing an unexpected and enormous demand for cash collateral on the company. The need to meet this demand can then throw the company into a liquidity crisis that may, in some cases, trigger still more downgrades. It all becomes a spiral that can lead to a corporate meltdown.

Derivatives also create a daisy-chain risk that is akin to the risk run by insurers or reinsurers that lay off much of their business with others. In both cases, huge receivables from many counter-parties tend to build up over time. A participant may see himself as prudent, believing his large credit exposures to be diversified and therefore not dangerous. However under certain circumstances, an exogenous event that causes the receivable from Company A to go bad will also affect those from Companies B through Z.

In banking, the recognition of a "linkage" problem was one of the reasons for the formation of the Federal Reserve System. Before the Fed was established, the failure of weak banks would sometimes put sudden and unanticipated liquidity demands on previously-strong banks, causing them to fail in turn. The Fed now insulates the strong from the troubles of the weak. But there is no central bank assigned to the job of preventing the dominoes toppling in insurance or derivatives. In these industries, firms that are fundamentally solid can become troubled simply because of the travails of other firms further down the chain.

You may read this and conclude, I don't know that I fully get everything Buffet was saying about derivative securities (in fact you may say I don't even know what derivative securities are—no worries), but you do see from just the underlined portions that he was highlighting the potential problems of these investment vehicles that appear to have materialized just as he described.

So paying attention to the economy is important in telling us what to do as well as what not to. This does not mean that suddenly everyone has to be an expert on complex financial topics such as derivative securities (not unless you want to; if you do, go for it). There are, however, a number of basic things we all can become familiar with regarding the economy that will be quite useful. I want you to take a closer look.

TIMES AND SEASONS

Prior to the recent Global Economic Crisis, most people were conditioned to believe that the economy pretty much only went in one direction—"up." In fact, popular 50-year charts of the stock market and other assets overtime were consistently pointed to because, despite the little dips in the squiggly line, they clearly demonstrated that the general trend was always up. In fact, it was accurately pointed out that one should not focus too much on the downward trends, because you might mistakenly jump out of the market at exactly the wrong time, missing the upward surge that would invariably ensue after a downturn. And while I am not here to buck conventional wisdom (or at least, not at this time), I do believe that if one interprets the conventional view of investing as, "I can pretty much ignore the economy because it always go up," we will miss much.

In *Wealth, Grow it God's Way*, we talked about the fact that one of the things Lord has established throughout His creation is this notion of "seasons." If we are aware of times and seasons, we are better able to understand where we are in life and what the next steps will be. The economy, in my view, is not exempt from this notion of times and seasons. It has seasons of growth, seasons of decline, and even seasons of stagnation.

Wisdom and understanding allows us to manage our finances and wealth in the context of what is going on in the economy, both in the short and long term. We cannot just assume that it is only going to move in one direction, whether good or bad. It may expand at a high growth rate for an extended period of time, but it is not going to continue forever at that rate. We have to understand that it can slow down and either level-off or enter a period of decline. We must position ourselves so that our portfolio of assets increases and our portfolio of liabilities decreases during these days of economic declines.

Goshen Principle #5: Be comfortable with the fact that the economy may move in other directions than just "upward." Also beware that while economic movements may come gradually, it is also possible that some may happen quickly. Have a game plan for how to act no matter what the direction or speed of the economy.

This was the challenge of America's recent housing crisis. When the real estate market and the economy went into decline, people found themselves in situations where their assets were decreasing while their liabilities were increasing, and doing so at a fairly rapid rate.

How did this happen? Well, as with any market drop, when the real estate market collapsed, the values of homes declined dramatically. Some people who bought real estate with the extreme enthusiasm that values would only increase, overpaid because they thought they would be able to quickly and easily "flip" the property or refinance it. But, as the market collapsed, they lost significant value in their assets. This, in and of itself, is not the biggest problem. It is easy to deal with a bad investment. You either wait until the value of the investment recovers or you sell and write off the loss. However, with the housing market there was another problem. Many had financed their real estate purchases with debt, so it was a little harder just to "write off" the investment.

This was not the only problem which was occurring. There were a number of investors who found themselves in a situation where their debt liabilities were not remaining flat, but instead, they were going up, because of financing decisions they had made. Unfortunately, there were a number of investors who financed their homes with mortgage instruments they did not fully understand—which, sadly, were starting to wreak havoc on their finances.

ANTHONY AND BRENDA

Take a look at Anthony and Brenda. This couple was married with two children, renting a 2-bedroom apartment, and working to get themselves established financially after finishing college. They had slowly worked their way into solid positions on their jobs. Recently, they had heard a lot about how they could finally realize their dream of owning a home and having more space for their children because lenders were being lenient with the amount needed down on a house and credit requirements. So they thought that with both incomes they might be able to qualify.

Anthony and Brenda talked with a mortgage broker, John, who reassured them that not only was this the best step for building long-term wealth, but he was confident that he could get them qualified for a loan from one of the many companies that he dealt with on a daily basis. It turns out John was right. They were able to qualify for a loan and in a few short months, they were moving into their first home. Everything seemed perfect.

Then came 2008 and Anthony was laid off from his job. With both incomes, their finances were tight, but manageable. Now, with Anthony out of work, they found themselves dipping into their savings just to make ends meet. Matters became worse when Brenda's company started cutting back overtime and announced that people were going to have to take unpaid furloughed days to deal with the economic downturn. Despite it all, Anthony and Brenda felt they could make it. They were going to have to figure out how to replace the money that they had begun saving for the children's college, yet they knew things would get better eventually.

If this was not enough, they opened the mortgage bill and found that the mortgage payments had jumped significantly. They called their broker, John, to see if there was something he could do to get them into a different mortgage. Their efforts were futile. With the down market, their investment had lost significant value due to the distressed home sales in the area and banks were hesitant to refinance, even though Anthony and Brenda had struggled to make their mortgage payments on time each month. What were they going to do now?

"MY BROKER SAID"

On the surface, it would seem like a smart move to use an adjustable rate mortgage (ARMs) as a debt financing strategy just before a financial crisis. Why? Because, the typical adjustable rate mortgage is pegged to a bank interest rate like the Prime lending rate or LIBOR rate, which during economic downturns actually decline. But if you read the fine print, the ARMS that Anthony and Brenda had were not what I will call "traditional ARMs." They were not tied to bank rates.

Instead, they were pegged to <u>pre-determined schedules</u> that were set to <u>increase at a given interval no matter what was going on in the economy</u>. With this feature, lenders flooded the sub-prime market with these loans because it increased their ability to generate profits, making markets that historically had higher risk and lower returns much more attractive.

On the other side of this transaction, were the entities willing to lend money (knowingly or unknowingly) under this system. These securities were perfect for individual and institutional investors that wanted to lock in favorable returns. Unfortunately, however, these securities turned out to be "weapons of mass destruction" for the borrowers and lenders.

These "new kinds of ARMs" (I'll use this term to distinguish them from "traditional" ARMs) and other mortgages that were often sold in mass to "sub-prime borrowers" who probably did not fully understand the *economic risks and ramifications* of what they were getting into).

Such mortgages were also probably sold by too many brokers that may have or may not have understood the risks and ramifications of these loans either. I personally remember hearing far too many people repeat the refrain, "My broker said that I could refinance my loan in a year and get into a fixed rate loan."

So sadly, when the real estate market collapsed, some of the borrowers saw their monthly mortgage payments (payments that were probably a little to steep to begin with) increasing. This happened even while their home values were decreasing, and while their personal income was on a downward spiral due to layoffs, pay freezes, and cut-backs.

Understanding how their loan would perform in various economic circumstances would have helped these individuals make much better borrowing decisions *(we will discuss this more later).*

Goshen Principle #6:

- Take time to understand how the changing economic environment will or will not affect your finances and investments.
- Try to include assets that have the ability to move with the economic cycles as well as assets that run counter to such cycles (i.e., they hold or increase in value when the economy is declining).
- But, in all cases, if you are using debt to acquire an asset, avoid using debt which increases even when the economy, your assets, your income, and your cash flow are declining.

Brian's Choices

On the other hand, there were positive things happening during this time for some individuals. There were those who had a better grasp of the economy and that were, in fact, able to make more optimal financing decisions.

I remember talking to a gentleman named Brian. He was considering refinancing options for his home and was choosing between a fixed rate and a "traditional" adjustable rate mortgage. Brian and his wife researched the market thoroughly and decided to go with the "traditional" ARM, which had a rate pegged to one of the prime lending rates because they felt pretty certain that with everything going on, the economy was going to begin to decline.

All of the signals, for them, seemed to be pointing to an imminent economic slowdown. Brian felt that he would save thousands of dollars by using a traditional ARM. After the economy declined, his plan was to lock in a fixed rate mortgage that would be lower. They figured that even in a worse case scenario, they should be able to qualify for a loan because they were not going to use the equity in their home to get into a larger one as their broker had encouraged. Instead, they were going to leave the equity alone because they felt they lived in a stable community that did not experience a lot of turnover.

It turns out that Brian and his wife were "spot on." They probably saved not only thousands of dollars, but perhaps tens of thousands, by rightly assessing the economic context of his investing and financing decisions.

I also want to point out that Brian's decisions were not without risk. It was completely possible for the economy to expand at a faster rate instead of declining. In this case, they would have been stuck with higher interest rates, higher borrowing costs, and thus more debt. Being that Brian and his wife were diligent watchers of the economy, they felt they could continue to monitor it for any sharp movements in a new direction.

So how do you monitor the economy? How can we have more insight and understanding of the situation? Our example in the story, Brian, was not an economist and neither was his wife. He was just a hard working guy on "the nine-to-five" like everyone else, and his wife was a "stay-at-home mom." What they had both done over time was develop a working knowledge of some of the basic economic indicators that help us understand the "*seasons* of the economy."

CHAPTER 3

THE EXPENDITURE MODEL

Another one of the hats I wear is that of adjunct professor at one of the area universities. I teach Macroeconomics and Global Economics, and one of the many things I love about the topic of Economics is that there are simple models that can be very useful in understanding the financial world around us.

A basic model that people following the economy often use is the *Expenditure Model*. Some of you may remember this from economics class or *perhaps have permanently blocked it from your memory bank*. Specifically, it is the measure of GDP (gross domestic product—(i.e., the nation's economic output) using the expense method (i.e., how everyone is spending money). I believe one of the reasons that it is so common is because it is simple and useful. I could take time to go through other models and ways of looking at the economy, but I if we went into them here, you might want to immediately slam this book down or shut off your eReaders. So instead, let's keep things fun and focus only on this intuitive model of the economy.

If I were to put it in completely simplistic terms, I would say the model goes something like this:

The economy is made up of four things:

1. Consumers (C) who are buying "stuff."
2. Businesses (I) that are buying "stuff."
3. The Government (G) which is buying "stuff."
4. And net exports (E) – the stuff we sell to other countries (exports) *minus* the stuff we buy from other countries (imports).

Some of you may now remember the mathematical equation that follows:

$$C + I + G + X = \text{Economy (GDP)}$$

This equation is quite intuitive. It basically tells us that to understand the total value of the economy, we add up the four areas.

Allow me to make an important note. Going back to my simplification of Business and Government spending, it is important to highlight that Business and Government spending is slightly different than Consumer spending. Business spending actual refers to **investments** that are made such as equipment, machinery and plants. We do not include business inventory costs or residential construction because this is included in the Consumer spending numbers.

Similarly, Government spending refers to things such as infrastructure, public buildings, military weapons, and civil servant salaries, but it would not include transfer payments which are outlays for things such as unemployment, social security or welfare payments because these are accounted for in the Consumer numbers.

Whew! Okay—so this is all of the economics we need to master to begin to manage our financial lives more effectively. Like the farmer, we can use this model to better understand the "weather conditions" a.k.a. "the economic conditions." This then helps us better weigh the types of actions that make the most sense for us in the short and long run.

So using this formula, let's see what we now know about the economy?

#1: We know the economy is growing when:

- Consumers are buying more stuff,
- Businesses are investing in more stuff,
- The Government is buying and building more stuff,
- (...and this is the tricky one) The nation is selling more stuff to other countries than it is buying from other countries.

#2: The other side of this coin is that we know the economy is shrinking when:

- Consumers buy less stuff or stop buying all together,
- Businesses invest less or postpone investments altogether.
- The Government is buying and building less,
- The nation is buying more stuff from other countries than it is selling to other countries.

Hopefully, at this point, everything is starting to become clearer. Basically, by using this model of the economy, we do not have to wait until the NBER (National Bureau of Economic Research) announces the start or end of a recession to begin to understand what is going on in the economy. And yes, we can do more than the old economist joke that says, "A recession is when your neighbor loses his job, a depression is when you lose yours."

We carefully observe the things around us, and now we can combine this with information about the economy.

The next question is how do we get simple and "digestable" economic information which we can use to inform our financial decisions without being overwhelmed?

The answer is quite simple. We have to do three things. First, categorize the type of information about the economy you would like to know. Second, determine the sources of data that you will use. And third, develop a schedule for when you will "pay attention" or review the facts.

Goshen Principle #7:

- You do not have to absorb the myriad of economic information that is out there. Simply choose a few basic statistics that you will follow at least on a semi-annual basis.
- The expenditure model of the economy can be an easy way to select a few data elements that may be helpful.

I recommend that you start by breaking economic data into five categories: Overall Economy, Consumers, Business, Government, Net Exports. Table 1.0, shows a simple approach that you can use for your plan.

Table 1.0

	Impact to Economy	Economic Information	Source	Type of Indicator
Overall Economy		Semi-annual Monetary Report to Congress	Federal Reserve	
Consumers	70%	Consumer Confidence Index (monthly)	University of Michigan	Leading
Business	15-20%	Durable Goods Orders	Bureau of Census	Leading
Government	15-20%	U.S. Deficit	U.S. Treasury	
Net Exports	- (10-15)%[1]			

1. Yes, this is negative because th U.S. imports more than it exports, which creates a trade deficit.

THF FED

The first category is information regarding the state of the overall economy.

In America, there is no shortage of opinions and analyses regarding how the economy is performing. In fact, there is a dizzying amount of data from academia to media, from financial institutions to politicians. Everyone is constantly weighing in with the definitive perspective on the economy. And during election seasons, this only gets worse as each candidate or party tries to advance their specific agenda. But I think the best source of objective, even-handed information regarding the economy is The Federal Reserve Bank (The Fed).

As the central bank of the United States, one of the Fed's responsibilities is to do its part to ensure a stable U.S. economy.

Twice a year, the Chairman of the Fed testifies before Congress to give his view of the state of the economy and the actions that he believes are or are not necessary to move the economy forward. This is done in the *Semiannual Monetary Policy Report to the Congress*.

Every six months is a good interval to step back and assess where the overall economy is headed. Anything more frequent may cause one to be overly obsessed with the short-term fluctuations that occur. Also, because the Fed Chairman is testifying before congress there are a lot of very easy ways to get this information including:

- Summaries from the national media
- Articles from newspapers and Internet websites
- Full coverage via sources like CSPAN

- Transcripts from the Federal Reserve website

The Fed has numerous economists and statisticians crunching numbers. Getting this data can be as simple as waiting until February or July of each year for the Chairman to make his presentation to Congress, and then turning on the news.

From a business perspective, it is akin to the President giving the State of the Union address, just with more detail and without the partisan applause. Another thing you can do (if you are increasingly finding the area of economics fascinating) is to go to the website for the Federal Reserve and pour through their reports (www.federalreserve.gov).

CONSUMER CONFIDENCE

The second category in Table 1.0 is *economic information about Consumers*. Many years ago, when I was a senior in college, I, along with some other students, were offered the chance to be interviewed by CNN (which was not quite the household name that it is now) to give our view on the economy and how it was impacting the job market. At the time, another school from the Big Ten, the University of Michigan, was releasing their Consumer Confidence Index.

It was starting to show that Consumer Confidence was continuing to fall which meant that the economy was going to slow down and graduating seniors were going to have increasing difficulty finding jobs. Fortunately, the effects had not really begun to make its impact. For us, it was just a cool opportunity to be interviewed. But for me, it became a time of increasing anxiety because an interview that was only supposed to take an hour or so, actually took up several hours and began seriously eating into the time I needed to study for my International Finance final exam.

It's rather humorous when I look back on it. I was so concerned about my exam that when we were finished, I zipped back to my dorm to "hit the books" and forgot to notify my family of the CNN interview in advance. Later on that evening, not realizing how fast the news cycle was that what I specifically said was captured, I received a call from my mother saying that several of her friends had contacted her stating that they had seen me on CNN. She clearly wanted to know what that was about since the only thing that I was supposed to be doing was studying for finals. Even my friend's dad in Atlanta called saying he saw me on the news. (Oops! That went over well. Note to self, tell family of interview in advance.)

Back to the subject. Consumer Confidence is a

great data source and there is much we can learn from this economic information.

As we know, consumer spending is the biggest driver of the U.S. economy, representing about 70% growth. So the Consumer Confidence Index is giving us data concerning one of the most important aspects of the economy. Another cool thing about this index is that it is what we call a "**leading indicator**," meaning it gives us a clue what could happen in advance.

In my case, the impact of the falling Consumer Sentiment did not hit our graduating class immediately, but it did about six months later, as the recession began to gain full stride. Which brings up another point that I will insert here.

The Impact of Employment

Many times people look at reports on jobs as a way of understanding the economy, which is a good thing. The U.S. Department of Labor has the Bureau of Labor Statistics, which publishes a great deal of data concerning the nation's population including the rate of employment and unemployment.

The challenge with looking at unemployment statistics is that while it is a fairly simple concept that we all relate to either as employees trying to keep jobs or as employers making decisions about jobs (or both), it is a **lagging indicator**.

Let's go back to my earlier story from college. By the time the graduating seniors were finishing their collegiate careers, there were signs that the economy was starting to lose ground. However, as clear as the indications may have been, one of the last things to be impacted was jobs. Why was that? Well let's think through a simple scenario.

Consumers start to lose confidence in the economy and begin to cut back on spending. Companies notice that consumers are buying less, so they cut back on production (initially just decreasing worker hours). As the cycle of decreased spending continues, companies realize that they have to cut back more and thus begin to layoff workers.

We can also look at the opposite scenario.

Consumers grow more confident in the economy and begin to increase the spending. There were a number of purchases which they had delayed because they wanted to be sure that they were not going to be caught "short on cash" when it was needed most. With the end of the recent war, however, consumers feel like there is less turmoil in the world. They feel pretty certain that the economy is not going to get any worse, so they begin buying again.

Corporations notice that consumers are purchasing more, but before they hire additional people, they are going to use up the excess inventories they have on hand. They are also going to see how much they can grow by just having the existing employees work smarter and harder. After a few quarters, it becomes clear that the upswing in consumer demand is solid and to avoid missing future growth, companies begin hiring additional workerfs.

Both scenarios show us that employment, both increases and decreases, is a lagging indicator of what is going on in the economy.

This is another reason why during political campaigns, I put very little weight on rhetoric about unemployment. It takes time for employment to turn (positively or negatively). It is like the caboose of a train. If you want to get it going in the right direction, it is more important to focus on the engine.

For example, I remember watching former President George H. W. Bush when he was running for re-election. On this particular day, someone in the media asked him about the economy. He responded by basically saying that there was not a whole lot that he could do because we were in a global recession.

Many did not like his answer, but I always thought

that he gave the most honest and accurate response. Truthfully, there was not much he could do to immediately impact the economy and job growth.

As an economics student, I had a chance to see the numbers. It was true, it was going to take time to work through it. Presidential candidate Bill Clinton, however, picked up on the fact that people felt the need for a better answer, and based his campaign for President using the slogan "It's the economy, stupid." It worked in getting him elected, but it did not make President Bush's statement any less truthful.

Americans obviously felt better voting for someone who recognized that the economy was important to them.

During the 2012 presidential election cycle "the economy" and "jobs" dominated the headlines once again. I am not a political scientist and I do not have an opinion about which candidate or party has the "right politics." I do believe, however, from an economic perspective that coming out of the "greatest recession in the last 70 years," it is unreasonable to believe that there should have been or even could have been any meaningful job "growth"—especially when you look at:

1. Hundreds of billions of dollars (a Bloomberg news teams actually put the number in the trillions)

going to stave off a near collapse in the global financial system, which means that consumers would not only have lost confidence in the economy but in the financial institutions that support it.

2. Two wars in the Middle East, and more threats and conflicts elsewhere, which means that consumers have greater uncertainty about the future.

3. Technology innovation which is redefining employment in such new ways that many jobs are being outsourced or permanently eliminated, meaning that many consumers have decreased confidence about tomorrow because they have been displaced in the short term.

When you have all these things going on—and this is just the tip of the iceberg—it is easy for us to understand the current direction of the economy.

For me, after looking to the Federal Reserve to see what actions it chooses to take, the next institution one could look to is the United States Congress.

THE WAR IN WASHINGTON

Our Congress has the ability and responsibility of enacting fiscal policy that benefits the nation's economy, among other things. Unfortunately, in recent months and years, fighting, both within political parties and across party lines, has all but immobilized this institution and prevented it from enacting coherent legislation which will aid the economy.

- One group insists we must lower taxes to help the economy, another group says we need to raise them.
- One group says, decrease federal spending to help the economy, another says, this is absolutely the wrong time to decrease federal spending, matters will only get worse.
- One group says, having national healthcare will hurt the economy, while another group says, reforming the nation's healthcare is absolutely essential—and will result in economic growth.

The constant debate may cause a person to become discouraged about the U.S. economy, but I would caution against weighing the productivity of Congress too heavily. Fiscal policy is an inherently political, and thus a difficult and time-consuming area to wade through. (In fact, this is one of the downsides for those who take a strong Keynesian view of the economy—by the time legislators act, it may be too little, too late). It's okay to use congressional and political debates to understand perception regarding the factors that could be most heavily influencing the economy, but draw your own conclusions based on prayer and wisdom.

THE ROLE OF BUSINESS

The third category is economic information about business spending. Just like the other categories, there is no shortage of data regarding business activity in the economy. A simple measure that we can use is called **durable goods orders.**

Durable goods or "hard goods" as they are also known, are not items that you cannot consume at once—such ice cream or paper towels. A durable good typically lasts three years or more, like automobiles, central air conditioning units, or refrigerators. I like the durable goods order measure because once again it is rather intuitive.

When people and businesses are uncertain about the economy, they become more conservative in their buying decisions. Larger and more costly expenditures are delayed until they are absolutely necessary. Why spend a lot of money replacing a washing machine, if you can buy some time and save money by simply having it repaired? The extra money can be used to create a cushion during the tight times.

As consumers are more confident in their future and have more money to spend, they go ahead and purchase those much-needed items. Meanwhile, manufacturers of durable goods follow the same cycle. They are not going to spend valuable capital investing in equipment and plant capacity if they do not have a healthy amount of orders for these products.

Businesses will delay investment until they are absolutely certain that their commitment to manufacturer the durable goods will result in sustained growth.

Each month, the Bureau of Census of the U.S. Department of Commerce produces a report of durable goods orders. You can get the information from your favorite business newspaper like the *Wall Street Journal* or you can go online. Also if you follow business news via radio or television, many programs will provide an update of the durable goods order statistics each month. Listen to the updates as they are released, but do not get caught up in the month-to-month fluctuations. Instead, look at the longer term of at least 6 to 12 months in the context of the other economic data.

DEALING WITH THE DEFICIT

A simple place we can look to understand how the U.S. Government is spending money is to the United States Treasury.

We talked earlier about how politicized the topic of "jobs" and "unemployment" can be. If there is anything that has recently been even more politicized than "jobs," it has been the U.S. deficit. <u>The deficit is</u>

the amount by which the government expenditures exceed government revenues (i.e., taxes).

The deficit is important because it gives us a view of whether or not the government is spending more than it is collecting. In the fall of 2011, the U.S. deficit exceeded $1 trillion.

Many people use the terms deficit and debt interchangeably, and while they are related, they mean two different things. The deficit is the revenue shortfall based on current spending. I equate this to a person over-drafting his or her checking account. If the U.S. is running a deficit, then this will need to be made up with borrowing, which leads us to the national debt—the amount that the government owes.

Recently, with spending on multiple wars, the financial crisis, tax cuts, and various other items on the domestic agenda, the U.S. finds itself with one of the largest levels of national debt in its history, when you measure it as a percentage of the overall economy.

The February 29, 2012 Monthly Statement of the Public Debt of the United States, placed the national debt at $15,488 Trillion. If we use the end of 2011 numbers for GDP that was produced by the Bureau of Economic Analysis of $15.3 Trillion, it means that the national debt is currently more than 100% of the U.S. economy.

An Earthquake Ahead?

In our Goshen framework of building wealth, this would clearly indicate that the "weather conditions" for the U.S. economy are sub-optimal. It would not take much for one to get the ominous feeling that there is a 9.0 earthquake rumbling, a category 5 hurricane brewing, both to be topped off with a barrage of tsunamis and tornadoes that will level the U.S. economy. Anyone living in this country has probably already felt the reverberations of the faltering economy without even looking at the specific report, but the data helps us get a more complete picture of the situation.

So what exactly should be done? Many are currently pounding the table and saying that action is needed now—which almost everyone would agree. How should we assess the deficit data, and develop our opinion about the right course of action?

One side says, "Increase taxes to make up for the revenue shortfall." The other says, "No, cut government spending because it is too large, we don't need more government." This reverts back to the other side, which insists, "In a down economy, this is the wrong time to cut spending because the government is helping to prop up a fragile economy. Instead, let's raise taxes because they were cut too much previously."

To which the other side responds, "You can't raise taxes on those who are most responsible for growing the economy."

We could go on and on, take up a lot of space, and not make much progress.

THE PROFESSOR

One of my undergraduate economic professors was a man named Dr. Robert Eisner. Among other things, he was known for his view on federal deficits. In the mid 1980s, many were starting to become concerned about the government deficits that President Reagan was building up due to the large amount of spending on defense and tax cuts to the wealthy. (Wow, as Ecclesiastes states, there really is *"nothing new under the sun."*)

While some important economists were highlighting how pressing of an issue this was, Professor Eisner was saying, it may not be quite the big deal that everyone was making it out to be.

I distinctly remember the first time I heard Professor Eisner suggest to our class that the growing federal deficit and national debt was "not a problem" (at least not yet). There was a collective gasp that went through the entire lecture hall of about 200 students. We were like, "You have got to be kidding me! This guy is clearly 'off his rocker!'"

How could he possibly think that a government spending more than it was taking in was reasonable?" With the perplexed look that was on my face, I was clearly among them.

Over the next several classes, Professor Eisner laid out his argument and analysis about federal deficits. It was also not uncommon to read one of his opinions in the Economy section of a major paper such as the *New York Times* or the *Wall Street Journal*.

While I do not totally embrace the notion of overspending by the government, Professor Eisner taught me some valuable lessons about taking too much of a "knee jerk reaction" to the topic of Federal deficits. A point he highlighted was that in times of crisis—when consumer spending has collapsed, business spending has stopped, and tax revenue to the treasury has dried up—the government may need to play a critical role in keeping the economy moving through deficit spending. In fact, if the government stops spending right when every sector of the economy needs help the most, it could exacerbate the situation and cause a collapse.

In his view, the government should use its power to borrow money and prop up the economy until it recovers. Then it can more easily fill deficits and pay down debts.

In fact, the Federal Reserve has followed a similar policy throughout the crisis in saving the financial system which was beginning to crumble. Chairman Bernanke, who was an expert economist on the Great Depression, realized that the U.S. was in a similar situation in 2008.

The big mistake the Feds made before the Depression, to oversimplify, was that they stopped helping the banking system when it needed the most help, and as result, the U.S. entered the Great Depression. The chairman purposed not to allow the country to make the same mistake again and instead worked with the U.S. Treasury to enact unprecedented measures to help the system, which most would agree is working.

So what exactly should be done now regarding deficits and the national debt? Here is how I look at the matter.

I believe that right now our nation needs a great deal of prayer and wisdom to choose the prudent path forward. There is no quick fix. It took time to get into this mess and it will take time to get out. Also, the time when we should have worked aggressively on the deficit was during the "times of plenty." In the "lean times," the aggressive deficit reductions and austerity measures can exacerbate the very problem that we must solve.

The road forward needs to include asking everyone along the socio-economic continuum to contribute—or I dare say "sacrifice"—so that, in the end, everyone will benefit appropriately. If we do not act as "One nation under God," as our Pledge of Allegiance suggests, we will not be a nation that is "indivisible."

Prayerfully watch not just the level of the U.S. deficit, but how well people work together to address the problem. I believe that the body of Christ can help our nation pull out of this crisis both spiritually and naturally, but only if we do not get caught up in the political fighting ourselves. If feel the body of Christ must not allow itself it to be divided through partisan rhetoric or politics. Remember Ephesians 4:4-6 tells us: *"There is* ***one*** *body and* ***one*** *Spirit, just as you were called in* ***one*** *hope of your calling;* ***one*** *Lord,* ***one*** *faith,* ***one*** *baptism;* ***one*** *God and <u>Father of all</u>, who is above all, and through all, <u>and in you all</u>."*

THE CURRENT ACCOUNT

The final variable we can look at to assess the overall economy is Net Exports, which is also known as the Current Account.

If the U.S. is exporting more that it is importing, then it has a Current Account Surplus. If we are importing more than we are exporting, then we have a Current Account Deficit.

Over the recent years, our nation has been running a current account deficit, especially with countries like China. So in our Goshen framework, how should we review this data? Personally, I think it is good indicator to follow so that we understand how our nation is interacting in the global economy. Ideally, we would like to export more than we import, but on the other side of that equation, is that part of how developing economies are getting stronger is by learning how to manufacture goods that they can sell to the rest of the world.

Clearly, until those economies grow larger and stronger, they are probably going to sell us more than they can buy from us in return. We will obviously clearly need to watch this to ensure that we are in balance.

The Current Account also tells us how well we are saving. You can view the Current Account not just as the difference between exports and imports, but the difference between public consumption and public saving. Unfortunately, over the last thirty years, the

U.S. has gone from being a nation of savers to being a nation of spenders. We have probably done as much to get our own selves in trouble as any other institution that we may look to cast the blame upon.

Summary Action Steps:

- Take time to pay attention to key economic indicators. Pick a few to understand and follow.
- Twice a year, sit down and assess all of the key indicators that you follow. What do they tell you about the economy?
- Update your financial and investment approach, to take into account your current view of the economy.

CHAPTER 4

TIME FOR SEED-GATHERING

If we look at the inner portion of the GoWeM Framework, we see what I refer to as the four seed process: *Gather, Manage, Grow, and Leverage.*

These four processes sit on the inside of the circle

to remind us that everything we do to obtain, manage, and increase wealth happens in varying economic environments, both positive and negative.

This is the Economic Context that we talked about in the previous chapter. But all of these processes, including the Economic Context, sit inside of the main circle—the Spiritual Context—reminding us that everything is superseded by what happens in the Spirit. In this chapter, we will take a closer look at the first step: **Gather Seed.**

Gathering seed is the process of obtaining money or acquiring assets. In chapter 1 we talked about the fact that we do not actually "create" wealth ourselves, but we tap into it. So, in reality, *gathering seed* is the process by which we tap into the wealth that God has for us. There are three ways to obtain seed:

1. Inheritance

If you look at a list of some of the wealthiest people, you will often see several individuals who are there because of inherited wealth. While many of us would love to be in that position, at this point, it is probably not something we have control over.

2. Business Income

Obtaining income from a business, whether full-time or part-time, can be an excellent source of financial independence. This may not always be the easiest thing, but it certainly can be one of the most rewarding.

3. Working on a Job

In this chapter, we will focus on this because it is how most people generate incomes or *gather seeds.*

The question is: How do we become more effective in gathering seed? How do we increase the amount of seed that we gather?

In *Wealth, Grow it God's Way,* we outlined several Income Increasing Strategies that we can use on our jobs. Now, I want to build on those concepts and push our thinking a bit further. In doing so, I believe it can really liberate us as believers to be even more effective in our work, more productive in increasing the flow of income through those jobs, and ultimately being able to bless the Kingdom of God because of the increased giving that it enables.

Not long ago, my mother had a book whose title caught my attention. It was, *The Value of Work in the Eyes of God,* by Douglas Woolley. I flipped it over to the back cover and saw what I thought was a timely description.

> *"Practically every adult works in some way. Yet, many workers feel unfulfilled and frustrated*

in their work, including Christians. Those in secular employment often feel that they waste the majority of their time on things that really do not matter in the grand scheme of God.

While most understand that pastors, missionaries, and church workers perform work that is valuable to God, many do not realize that other work has value in God too."

I agree with Mr. Woolley; in fact, I would like to take it a step further. I believe that many of us do not realize what we are doing is not just valuable work, but it is actually ***His work***.

The problem with not realizing this is that we then fail to *maximize our potential* in that "ministry," which can cause us to miss valuable opportunities for the Lord to bless us with increased income through our job.

Some occupations are obvious "ministries," such as doctors, teachers, firemen, and social workers, just to name a few—but, I am not limiting our discussions to only those areas. I am also talking about the waitress and the bus driver, the billing representative and the computer repair person—all of these are examples of ***His work*** that God can call us to.

Whatever we are doing, we must see that work as our ministry. When we do, our entire thought processes regarding that endeavor will change.

Let me clarify what I mean. I am not referring to how we can spend time on our jobs witnessing and telling people about the love of Jesus Christ. This is fine, but in some environments it is not possible and could result in negative consequences. I am also not just talking about how we can quietly "let our lights shine" so that through our actions and the way we treat our co-workers, people understand we are "different" and thus want to learn more about Jesus. Yes, this is our "reasonable service," but I am really moving beyond even this point.

What I am speaking of is the fact that the talents you have and the job at which you do them, may actually be a divinely orchestrated environment at a given moment in time, or season in your life to prosper you.

MORE THAN MONEY

Let me share a personal example.

For the better part of sixteen years, I have been blessed to work as a management consultant. My area of focus has been in helping some of America's largest and most recognized financial institutions develop various business strategies to help them grow and become more effective in the market. Management

Consulting, as many of you can attest, is a very demanding and fast–paced job where turnover is extremely high. Some statistics say that nearly 50% of new management consultants do not make it beyond their third year. And when other factors such as gender and race are taken into account, the statistics become even more lopsided, with a much smaller percentage of females, or in my case, African-American females, staying in the field. And when you look at the number of African-American females that go on to become partners in their firms, those statistics are even more stark.

So why did it work for me? It is clear that it was divine intervention which placed me at a really great firm that was a perfect fit for me. I loved the people and I loved the work. But I have to admit that I actually did not stay through the years and work all of those crazy hours, long weekends, traveling across the country, and even outside of the country, sleeping in all kinds of hotels, airports, and airplanes, because I loved the people and work—as cool as they were. In fact, truth be told, there were many days when I honestly **did not** love it, but stayed anyway. Why? Was it for the money? No. I made up my mind a long time ago that I would not make myself miserable and sick working in an environment that I couldn't stand, **just for the money**. Instead, I would trust God for something else, leave and do without, if necessary.

No, I did it, and enjoyed the process, because I actually felt that *I was working in the place where God wanted me. I felt that I had been given a mission by Him to help clients make their businesses better and grow them, thus creating more jobs and incomes for their employees, a strong tax base for their respective communities, etc.*

This belief about my mission guided me during challenging times, like the days when I had to work with executive leadership teams to build alignment on important business decisions. In those moments I quietly prayed for the wisdom to listen, how to hear their concerns, and how to find the path that would bring them together. I had to. It was my ministry assignment. The livelihoods of a number of people and their progeny could be directly impacted by how well I performed my job, and by how well my team did theirs.

This is just as important as the evangelist who does not give up on the wayward teenager, or the pastor who works to help pull a couple through a difficult patch in their marriage. It's all ministry. It is all *His work.*

In the late night hours, when I was extremely tired and wanted to give up, I could feel the Holy Spirit nudging me on to finish the task, to "finish my course," as the Apostle Paul would say. I had to seek God for *His answers,* because the well-being of His people was on the line.

When I was seemingly too exhausted to even feel the Holy Spirit, I had my mother there to encourage me and let me know that the Lord was with me. Yes, I was physically drained, but I could keep going. God would always be faithful.

This is my story, but I am sure there are numerous others who can share experiences of how they were able to excel and thus increase their income. They did not achieve because they pushed, shoved, and elbowed to get ahead. Instead, they reached their potential because they walked in excellence and love.

Goshen Principle #8 : When we are where God has us, doing what He calls us to do, it *is* ministry. And when we focus on *maximizing our ministry* in that place, then we can maximize our income— maximize our ability to Gather Seed.

So why do I highlight this as a path to increase income? Is it because I want to naively suggest that all we have to do is just "put our heads down and work hard"? Such a philosophy can certainly have plenty of merit in several situations. But no, that is not it. Instead it comes from years of observing the actions and behaviors of people in the work place.

I have had the opportunity to hold several positions or be on committees where we had responsibility for making hiring or promotion recommendations. When I look at what makes people consistently successful in increasing their income throughout their careers, points like the ones that we have been discussing here clearly emerge.

Alternatively, when you look at men and women who seem to stagnate or stumble along the path of increasing their income, there are some key mistakes that surface as well. Here are a few common mistakes I have seen people make.

1. *They accept jobs that they should not take, because they are making their selection largely based on which job pays the most.*

2. *They vie for positions and promotions because they want more money instead of making sure that it is the best fit for them and it is in God's perfect timing.*

3. *They stay in higher paying positions purely because they pay more, knowing deep inside that it is time to move on and explore exciting new opportunities, even if they pay much less.*

4. *They ignore unethical or suspect behavior because they do not want to threaten their paycheck or potential promotion. In the end, they were either let go, when "everything came crashing down," or stifled in their career because their leadership or integrity was brought into question.*

5. *They leave current jobs for "greener pastures" (a.k.a. promised promotions and positions elsewhere) before it was the right time, instead of staying where they were and being a little more patient. Eventually, they walked away from more opportunity than they ever actually realized elsewhere.*

I believe when we understand that we are all workplace ministers, it allows the Holy Spirit to give us a new energy concerning our work. For example, as a teacher, you are not just seemingly fighting uphill battles against unappreciative administrators, parents, or other officials, but you are being God's vessel to shape the minds and hearts of His precious children and intercede for their souls. When you do this in the most creative and innovative way possible, a number of other doors can open. For example:

- Administrators can see your talent and work to promote you and increase your compensation.
- Parents appreciate your extra energy and work harder to support you and develop a teacher appreciation fund.
- A student goes on to great success and through his or her endeavors funds a special fellowship for teachers.
- You write a book describing your creative teaching approaches which becomes a best seller.
- You develop a special website for teachers, using your creative teaching approaches and educators from around the world follow the website to learn from your ideas. You are now impacting lives and selling educational products in different languages and on several different continents.

Reflect

If you currently work on a job, stop for a moment and think about how you can take what you are doing now to the next level. Do not worry about whether your current bosses have the ability or the willingness to compensate you for the additional creativity that you will bring to the position. Remember, promotion comes from God. When we "raise our game" for Him, He will "dispatch a blessing to 'overtake us.'"

To me, the most effective way to increase our compensation and bonuses is to allow the Holy Spirit to guide us in how to effectively represent Christ in the workplace. And the really cool thing is that it can be done without taking a cape and pinning a large "SC" on your chest, announcing yourself as a Super Christian there to "personally save the world." Just focus on being used by God to make the highest impact possible.

Summary

As believers, the key is to be in the place where God wants us to be, and then "minister" to the fullest—having the most influence and creating the most value possible, for as long as He tells us. As we work at our jobs or look for new opportunities, we should not only ask ourselves, "What are my capabilities?" or "What are my areas of interest?"

We should also ask a more important question: "God how do you want me to use my talents and interest to make a company and its people better? How can my skills and interactions with clients and customers be used to uniquely meet their needs, solve their problems, and show them that Jesus loves them?"

Press for excellence, not for man's recognition. Push to bring creative energy in everything and then maximize all of the channels through which that creativity can have a positive influence on others. If we do this, we cannot help but be blessed by our Awesome Heavenly Father.

Our income will absolutely increase, if not "immediately" certainly "eventually." Be patient and wait for it. It always comes.

When we seek first the kingdom of God, <u>all of the other things are always added</u>.

Practical Application

- New Job/Position

If you are considering a job change, outline all of the practical benefits associated with each alternative opportunity (compensation, role, responsibilities, location, brand, etc.) and then rank them in priority. Now outline all of the "spiritual" or intangible benefits, such as the ways you will be able to grow personally or how much you can impact others. Again, rank them.

Ask the Lord where He wants you to be. Choose the job that gives you the most peace and where you feel you are in complete alignment with the will of God. In the end, it may be the highest paying job. It may not, but the Lord will confirm His will.

• Current Position

For some, you may not be considering a job change, which is fine. We can still give ourselves a personal tune-up to make sure that we are maximizing our "ministry" or maximizing our effectiveness.

Begin by outlining all of the ways you have contributed (whether it was noticed and rewarded or not).

Second, outline new ways that you can make a positive impact. Look not only at bosses or managers, but also think about how you can make your peers, support staff, and clients more successful.

Third, develop a strategy and a timeline for how you will produce the effect you have outlined.

Fourth, now put the plan aside and pray about it for a few days, asking God to give you wisdom.

Fifth, pick up the list again. Revise the order, the strategies, and the timeline based on the leading of the Holy Spirit.

CHAPTER 5

YOU'RE THE MONEY MANAGER

When I was growing up, my family would always go on these fun driving trips to various places throughout the U.S. From Starved Rock State Park to P-Town (Province Town) on Cape Cod, from Key West, Florida to Ruby Falls, Tennessee. Mom packed up the car, Dad mapped out the routes, and off we went. I loved it!

I always knew we were really on our way when, as soon as we crossed the Chicago city limits to travel through the rest of the Prairie State, we found ourselves "dab smack in the middle" of farmland; mile after endless mile of soybeans, corn, wheat, cows, horses and hogs—vast acreage dwarfing the urban metropolis.

Another detail that always caught my attention was those massive cylinders off in the distance, with "upside-down snow cones on top." I eventually learned that these were silos for storing farmers' grain.

MANAGING SEED

The second Seed Process in the GoWeM Framework is called *Managing Seed* which encompasses budgeting and saving. Like the farmer who has to manage the grain silos, it is not just about seeing how much grain one can store. The farmer has to decide the amount that needs to be planted vs. the amount that needs to be sold vs. the amount that needs to be stored for the future.

These are important business decisions, and as Proverbs 27:23–27 tells us, we can't be negligent in managing:

> *"Be diligent to know the state of your flocks, and attend to your herds; for riches are not forever, nor does a crown endure to all generations. When the hay is removed, and the tender grass shows itself, and the herbs of the mountains are gathered in, the lambs will provide your clothing, and the goats the price of a field; You shall have enough goats' milk for your food, for the food of your household, and the nourishment of your maidservants"* (Proverbs 27:23-27).

Selling too much may mean that the farmer does not have enough seed to plant for the next year or to feed the family. Over-hoarding could mean missed opportunities for profit in an up market or missed opportunities for investments in the future growth of the farm.

The metaphor of the grain silo is the perspective that we should have as we think about budgeting and saving. Effective budgeting and saving means that we have properly structured our finances to position ourselves to maximize both current and future opportunities and to manage current and future risks.

In *Wealth, Grow it God's Way*, we talk about the difference between "saving" and "investing." Saving is setting aside "seed" so that you have some for the future. The goal for this seed is "preservation." We want it to be stored safely "in the grain silo," at the right temperature and protected from the elements or any type of disaster.

This is different from the "seed" (or money) that you invest, because investing is putting seed at risk (i.e., planting it in the soil) with the expectation that you can earn a return which justifies and compensates you for the risk taken. Saving 10% is a popular target. But, for some of us, we first have to manage our finances so that we actually have something to save.

Managing Seed: Financial Structuring

This leads us to a key aspect of how we manage our seed—it involves Financial Structuring.

If we look at a company's income statement, we find that there are two parts: Revenues and Expenses. For many people, most of the time that they spend working on their budget is done on the Expense side as opposed to the Revenue portion. Why? Well, I have found two main reasons. The first is because so many individuals receive their incomes from fixed sources such as a paycheck from a job or pension, they feel there is not a lot that they can do to make significant changes in their revenue.

A cost-of-living raise, a bonus, maybe some overtime—all of those things are good, but many feel it does not really "move the needle" in terms of improving their financial situation. However, I believe this is precisely where we must focus our faith and energy to help us get to where we want to be financially. I will come back to this later.

The second main reason is that many people sense they have structural problems with the amount and type of expenses that they have—and they must do something about it quickly.

Several years ago, when we first produced our television program titled, "Help God, My Spending is Out of Control," it immediately became one of the three most popular programs that *Finance: According to Your Faith* has ever aired. The second most popular was a series on Debt.

Many viewers responded saying how it really helped them see the areas in their finances where their spending was triggering numerous problems, even when they were making more than enough money to cover their expenditures.

So if managing the expense portion of a budget is a big area of concern, *how do we better manage these expenses?*

Managing Seed Exercise #1: Make a complete list of all your expenses.

I have found that one of the best ways to get a sense for all of your expenses, is not just to sit down and go through your bills and financial commitments (e.g., be sure to include money owed to family members or friends, etc.). To get a true sense of your expenditures, you should grab a small memo pad and also track every single thing you spend your money on.

Managing Seed Exercise #2: Track your expenditures for two weeks.

When people complete this exercise, they often are surprised to see how much money they are spending on "little things" such as purchases from vending machines, at their favorite coffee shops, or for small "treats" for themselves. Writing this all down allows us to see just how much we are spending. It is often upwards of 30–50% more than you would guess if you were to estimate it in your mind.

Once people have a detailed list of their expenses, many immediately jump to making their action plan. But there is more work to be done before we move to that step.

Remember, just like the farmer managing the grain

silos, it isn't only about seeing how much grain you can store. It involves managing the current and future opportunities and risk. To do this, we must understand how much "flexibility" there is in your expenses.

So let's take a closer look, because "expenses are not all created equal."

Goshen Principle #9: Budgeting is about managing current and future opportunities and current and future risks.

I like to look at expenses in two ways: Fixed and Variable.

Fixed expenses are those that you absolutely must pay each month or there will be significant consequences. You have very little flexibility in the amount of the expenses or the timing, because these have largely been set in advance (*more than likely they are set by a contract*).

Examples of fixed expenses include things such as mortgages, automobile notes, student loans, etc. Failure to pay these could mean very unpleasant consequences such as foreclosure, repossession or garnishment of wages.

Variable expenses, on the other hand, are ones that you have the ability to decrease or eliminate all together by making changes in your consumption habits. Yes, there can be consequences if you fall behind or stop paying, but normally these are the type of things that you can live with and/or manage with far less detriment to your credit score. Examples of variable expenses include:

- *Mobile phone*
- *Electricity*
- *Cable television/satellite*
- *Eating out*
- *New wardrobe*
- *Gasoline*

Fallacy of Composition

In economics, there is a principle called the Fallacy of Composition. This is an important concept in Macroeconomics because it helps students avoid making the mistake of taking an individual example and applying it to the economy as a whole. The example that is often used to explain the Fallacy of Composition is the notion called "The Paradox of Thrift."

Basically the paradox points out that while individuals can increase their savings by reducing their expenditures (e.g, go shopping less often for shoes),he or she has to be careful not to extrapolate this for the entire economy.

There is a natural tendency for individuals to apply the same notion regarding their personal budget to the economy as a whole. They conclude that to help the economy, everyone should do exactly as they did—immediately decrease all additional spending and balance their budget the way that we as individuals balance our checkbook. But as we noted in chapter 2, this has side effects.

When governments decrease spending, this can mean the loss of jobs, some businesses that supply services and products to the government can lose valuable contracts, and state/local governments lose a significant source of funds—which causes the job loss and the business loss cycle to happen all over again on the state level. So the cutback in expenditures in the macroeconomic environment means that more people do not have money. With fewer resources, consumers *(remember consumers are the largest part of the economy)* stop their spending, which actually puts a greater drag on the economy.

All of these actions are a part of the paradox of applying an individual approach to the macro-economics environment. In this instance, it clearly has to be different.

If we look around the world today, this is another reason why people in countries like Greece and France are fighting some of the "austerity measures" that are instituted as a result of the Global Economic crisis. Even in the U.S., there are those who are taking a similar position regarding how the country works to decrease its enormous and growing debt.

Why do I bring up the notion of the Fallacy of Composition in the Variable Expense discussion? Is this part of my clandestine plan to get everyone to appreciate and apply economics in their everyday lives? Yes it is. But there is another reason!

It is because we can have "expense fallacies" when managing our money. And while these are not Fallacies of Composition, they are fallacies none the less.

Expense Fallacies

One of the mistakes people can make when managing their expenses is that they put too much emphasis on certain variable expenses. Instead of treating these expenses as things that can be decreased or eliminated, they wrongly conclude that they are fixed and immovable. And while the item is very important to them at that particular moment and they are absolutely committed to spending money on it "month-in and month-out," <u>it is not a fixed expense</u>.

For example, some women may view the money they spend at the hair or nail salon as a fixed expense.

In planning out their budget, they put these expenses right after their mortgage and their car note. Once again, as important as it may be, "if push comes to shove" even this "sacred cow" has to be placed on the chopping block.

On the other hand, I have seen men treat the money they spend on golfing as a fixed expense. The notion that they would go the entire summer without playing golf, or, if they did, they would only be limited to a few outings on the nearest public courses, is just absolutely unthinkable.

Managing Seed Exercise #3: Separate your expenses into fixed and variable (make sure that variable expenses do not seep into the fixed expenses column).

Now let's calculate the percentages associated with your budget, beginning with fixed and variable expenses.

- What is your fixed expense percentage?

$$\frac{\text{Fixed Expenses}}{\text{Total Expenses}} = \underline{\qquad}\%$$

- What is your variable expense percentage?

$$\frac{\text{Variable Expenses}}{\text{Total Expenses}} = \_\_\_\_\_\%$$

One of our goals is to make sure that variable expenses comprise a bigger portion of our total expenses. Why? Because, like the farmer, we want to plan not just for the good weather conditions and bountiful crops, but we want to prepare for times when weather conditions and crops are dismal. During the days when our income decreases significantly, we want to ensure that we have the ability to quickly decrease our expenses as well. This way we can maintain a sufficient cash flow—even if its less, it still can be adequate enough to get us through the tight times.

This was one of the challenges for millions when the housing market collapsed bringing on the Great Recession and the global economic downturn. Unfortunately for too many, their expenses were fixed at a level that assumed a higher income. For married couples this could have meant that they both needed to be working full-time to cover the mortgage and car payments. When the downturn occurred and one either lost his job or saw her business revenue decrease, the household did not have the flexibility to lower expenses to meet the significant decrease in income.

Goshen Principle #10: In times of plenty, if you increase your expenses as your income increases, make sure that more of the increase is in the form of variable expenses and not fixed expenses. This gives you the ability during lean times to quickly lower your expenses to match any decrease in income.

Now that we have looked at the percentages for fixed and variable expenses, let's examine the structure of the overall budget.

In chapter 5 of *Wealth, Grow it God's Way*, we talked about the components of the personal budget. It includes: True Income, Personal Operating Income (POI), Personal Net Operating Income (PNOI), and Profits. I am not going to review it again, instead I will assume that you have it "down pat." So let's advance to the next level and look at what I refer to as "target structures."

I find that looking at your desired target structure is a more effective way of managing your money than just a list of expenses because it enables you to concentrate on where you want to go, instead of constantly glancing in the rear view mirror. It also helps you avoid just looking at the individual expenses, and instead focus on the overall strategy that you are trying to employ.

Target Structure #1

Category	Percentage
Tithes	10%
Giving	
Other Giving	
Saving	10%
Investing	
Fixed Expense	50%
Variable Expense	30%

Target Structure #1 is for people who are in the beginning phases of Bible-based financial management. They are focused on ensuring that their finances are properly balanced by:

- Putting God first – paying tithes
- Establishing personal saving habits—consistent amount for "preservation purposes"

- Ensuring that fixed expenses do not exceed 50% of their PNOI (Personal Net Operating Income)
- Managing variable expenses so that they do not exceed 30% of the PNOI

Target Structure #2

Category	Percentage
Tithes	10%
Giving	5%
Other Giving	5%
Saving	10%
Investing	5%
Fixed Expense	35%
Variable Expense	25%

Target Structure #2 is for individuals who have already begun to master some of the principles of Bible-based financial management and are now moving to the next level.

- Giving is now a pillar in their finances—*they have moved beyond just paying tithes, but they also give offerings, "first fruits," and help with other ministry/outreach needs. They have also expanded their giving beyond the church to include giving to other institutions and efforts that help people. These can be donations to educational institutions, hospitals, youth organizations, etc.*

- They have expanded beyond saving to include investing—*and are beginning to earn a reasonable rate of return.*

- Fixed expenses *now only make up about a third of their PNOI. As a result, they have more flexibility to consider more progressive financial strategies.*

- Variable expenses *are completely manageable. They have fun and enjoy life but they are not wasteful or excessive in their expenditures.*

I like Target Structure #2. When you look at the percentages, you may think it does not appear to be that big of a difference—and you're right. But it's not the amount that matters initially. Of greater concern is the focus. If we stay on target and get our habits right, everything else follows.

When we start to demonstrate that we have a greater understanding and can handle more, then I believe the Lord is able to "channel" additional wealth through us to be a blessing. It doesn't begin when we have a million dollars or billions of dollars. It starts with how we structure our finances when we only have nickels, dimes, and quarters.

Target Structure #2 says, "I have moved from just living and existing to prioritized giving and investing," which puts me on the path to a better future.

A NEW MINDSET

Several years ago, I was talking with a fairly affluent friend about tithing. He too shared the sentiment that tithing is "a given," it's "a no-brainer." He then related a conversation he had with one of his "even more affluent friends."

His friend told him, "I am not trying to figure out how to give God 10% and live out of the 90%. I am trying to figure out how to give God 90% and live out of 10%"—Whoa!

Okay, that comment just totally reset the bar in my mind regarding what our true financial mission is. If we are talking about finances, yet we are stuck on the "10/90" *(God's portion vs. our portion)* part of the equation as opposed to the "90/10" part, we're missing the mark completely!

This new mindset helps us get to the next Target Structure:

Target Structure "T"

Category	Percentage
Tithes	10%
Giving	10%
Other Giving	10%
Saving	10%
Investing	30%
Fixed Expense	10%
Variable Expense	10%

Target Structure "T" represents the type of "**transitional structure**" we embrace when we begin to see our finances beyond ourselves and/or our current situation.

In Target Structure "T", we give more than we consume. We invest more for future efforts and for future generations instead of spending it all on ourselves, our wants, our needs.

It is in Target Structure "T" that we begin to position ourselves for Kingdom Stewardship.

When you look at Target Structure "T", however, another "divine ah-hah" hits you. And what's that? You were probably already thinking it? It goes something like this...

"There is no way that I can give 30% and invest 30% of my income. Even if I get my expenses down to the point where they are at the bare minimum, and even if I pay off a lot of my debt, there is no way anyone can live without 60% of my PNOI. I only make $_____ (fill in the blank)."

You're right! That's it! You can't! Now you see why I said earlier that when budgeting focuses only on how to manage expenses it is missing the most important part—*revenue!*

For many of us, we are not going to get where we need to unless we center on *generating revenue*. This brings us to the next Goshen Principle:

Goshen Principle #11: We have just as much power to increase revenue as we do to reduce expenses. We must use our faith and creativity to bring forth newer and potentially bigger resources.

Practical Application: Managing Seed

1. Go back through Exercises 1-3.
    - Track your expenses for two weeks.

- Create a detailed budget separating variable expenses and detailed expenses.
    - As you look at the variable expenses, which are ones that you should probably decrease or eliminate all together?
    - Look at your fixed expenses, are these the best use of your "seed"? Is it helping to position you for the future? If yes, perfect. If not, develop a plan to decrease or eliminate the fixed expenses?
    - Check the interest rates and other terms associated with any debt that you have. Make sure that you have the most favorable terms you can get.
- Look at your current budget structure and compare it to the Target Structures in this chapter. Which are you closest to now (1, 2, "T")? Which one do you want to be close to? (Feel free to create your own Target Structure.)

2. Build an annual budget.
    - Create a budget for each month of the year.
    - Make special note of months where you have "non-monthly" expenses occurring such as property tax payments (sometimes these are semi-annual payments), license renewal

(these can be annual), school tuition (sometimes there is a deposit), etc.

3. Build an annual budget for your *new Target Structure.*
   - Create a budget for each month.
   - Determine the month and year when you move from your current budget structure to your new target structure. Is it 6 months away? Two years away?
   - After you reach your new Target Structure, define what your next one will be.

4. Remember to set your revenue targets.
   - Determine the amount of revenue that you will need to move from your current budget structures to your new target structures.
   - Brainstorm ways that you could generate the new levels of additional revenue. Remember to only use *mountain-moving faith,* when you come up with your ideas.

CHAPTER 6

INCREASE, MULTIPLICATION, AND PRESERVATION

Increase is foundational to the whole notion of farming. One apple seed does not produce one apple. Instead, one apple seed produces an apple tree, which produces apples for an extended period of time.

One of the things I have learned over the years is that when you read the Bible from Genesis to Revelation, there are some recurrent principles, making it clear that the principles are true and telling us they are priorities for believers. I believe God's law of "increase" or "multiplication" is one of those principles.

It begins in Genesis 1:28: *"God blessed them and said to them, 'Be fruitful and increase in number; fill the earth and subdue it. Rule over the fish of the sea and the birds of the air and over every living creature that moves on the ground.'"*

Here we see that one of the very first directives given to us by God our Father was to *"be fruitful and increase."* We were not only to increase in number by bearing children, but we were to increase in dominion, and authority. The command was not only to fill the earth, but we were to subdue the earth and everything in it. Wow!

Another example is found in Matthew 25: 26-30:

> *"But his lord answered and said to him, 'You wicked and lazy servant, you knew that I reap where I have not sown, and gather where I have not scattered seed. So you ought to have*

> *deposited my money with the bankers, and at my coming I would have received back my own with interest. Therefore take the talent from him, and give it to him who has ten talents. For to everyone who has, more will be given, and he will have abundance; but from him who does not have, even what he has will be taken away. And cast the unprofitable servant into the outer darkness. There will be weeping and gnashing of teeth.'"*

This parable about the Kingdom of Heaven is one of my favorites and highlights several things. First, the master expected the servants to produce an increase even if it was as little as the interest on a bank savings account.

Second, the servant who had worked the hardest to increase his money from 5 talents to 10 talents, is the one who received the additional talent that the lord took from the lazy servant, emphasizing the notion that *"to everyone who has, more will be given."*

And third, the "unprofitable" servant did not get a hug and pat on the head to assuage his fears, instead he was cast into darkness. Double "Wow!"

Finally, if we read John 15:1-2, we see yet another example of the principle of increase: *"I am the true vine, and my Father is the gardener. He cuts off every branch in me that bears no fruit, while every branch that does bear fruit he prunes so that it will be even more fruitful."*

Here we discover that the standard and very lifeblood of God's children is to "increase." And when we are increasing, He doesn't just say, "Good job." Instead, He pushes, reshapes, and enhances us so that we produce even more. Alternately, if we fail to increase, He cuts us off and no longer allows our vine to abide in His vine. Why? Because, we are absorbing His nutrients—His life source—but we are not producing. Triple "Wow!"

When I began to understand that the very sign of my connection to the Father is productivity and increase, it reshaped my entire thinking and my approach to life. It also changed my view about money and wealth. Riches are not things we try to get so that we can store them in a barn and admire. Luke 12:16-21 lets us know that is not a good idea.

For the believer, we have two main missions, (1) to invest more and (2) to give more. When we invest, we reap a harvest, we take part of the bounty and give. Then we take another part and invest so that we will have even more.

When we reap the next harvest, which will be even bigger, we start the cycle all over again. We are called to increase—it is our mandate.

Exercise #1: Set aside some quiet time and go through the Bible to find other examples of the Principle of Increase (Bible study tools such as a concordance may be helpful in completing this exercise).

- *What other examples were you able to find? List each of them.*
- *Write out the additional insights that you gained from these scriptures.*
- *List three things that you are going to do differently because of this enhanced understanding of the Principle of Increase.*

PURE GOLD

Over the last several years, the price of gold has soared more than 150%. In 2007 an ounce of gold in U.S. dollars ranged in price from $620 to $1000. By 2011, this range had climbed to as high as $1600 - $1900. Driving this flock to gold was a desire by many to preserve the purchasing power of their money given the uncertainty in the global financial markets and the instability in the geopolitical world.

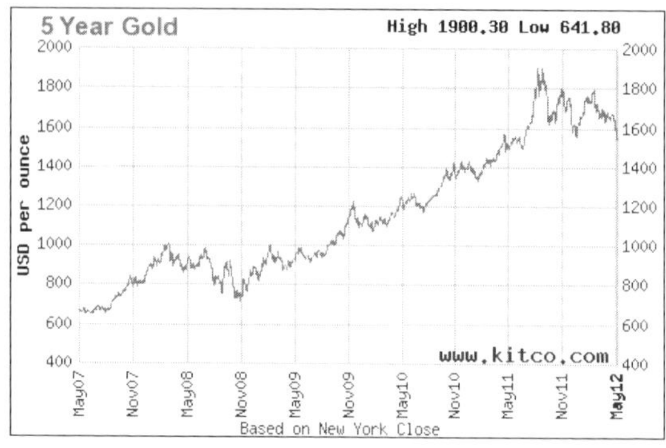

Warren Buffet, on the other hand, instead of rushing to gold as many had done, was doing just the opposite. In his view, the best defense against the loss of purchasing power was to invest in opportunities where he had the best chance for increase. In his mind this was stock.

Below is another great excerpt from a February 2012 *Fortune* article called, "*Warren Buffett: Why Stocks Beat Gold and Bonds.*" It is an adaptation of Mr. Buffet's shareholder letter.

Investing is often described as the process of laying out money now in the expectation of receiving more money in the future. At Berkshire Hathaway (BRKA) we take a more demanding approach, defining investing as the transfer to others of purchasing power now with the reasoned expectation of receiving more purchasing power—after taxes have been paid on nominal gains—in the future. More succinctly, investing is forgoing consumption now in order to have the ability to consume more at a later date....

Assets can fluctuate greatly in price and not be risky as long as they are reasonably certain to deliver increased purchasing power over their holding period. And as we will see, a nonfluctuating asset can be laden with risk....

Investments that are denominated in a given currency include money-market funds, bonds, mortgages, bank deposits, and other instruments. Most of these currency-based investments are thought of as "safe." In truth they are among the most dangerous of assets. Their beta may be zero, but their risk is huge.

Over the past century these instruments have destroyed the purchasing power of investors in many countries, even as these holders continued to receive timely payments of interest and principal. This ugly result, moreover, will forever recur. Governments determine the ultimate value of money, and systemic forces will sometimes cause them to gravitate to policies that produce inflation. From time to time such policies spin out of control.

Even in the U.S., where the wish for a stable currency is strong, the dollar has fallen a staggering 86% in value since 1965, when I took over management of Berkshire. It takes no less than $7 today to buy what $1 did at that time....

The second major category of investments involves assets that will never produce anything, but that are purchased in the buyer's hope that someone else.

This type of investment requires an expanding pool of buyers, who, in turn, are enticed because they believe the buying pool will grow still further. Owners are not inspired by what the asset itself can produce—it will remain lifeless forever—but rather by the belief that others will desire it even more avidly in the future.

The major asset in this category is gold, currently a huge favorite of investors who fear almost all other assets, especially paper money (of whose value, as noted, they are right to be fearful). Gold, however, has two significant shortcomings, being neither of much use nor procreative. True, gold has some industrial and decorative utility, but the demand for these purposes is both limited and incapable of soaking up new production. Meanwhile, if you own one ounce of gold for an eternity, you will still own one ounce at its end.

What motivates most gold purchasers is their belief that the ranks of the fearful will escalate. During the past decade that belief has proved correct. Beyond this, the rising price has on its own generated additional buying enthusiasm, attracting purchasers who see the rise as validating an investment thesis. As "bandwagon" investors join any party, they create their own truth—for a while.

Over the past 15 years, both Internet stocks and houses have demonstrated the extraordinary excesses that can be created by combining an initially sensible thesis with well-publicized rising prices. In these bubbles, an army of originally skeptical investors succumbed to the "proof" delivered by the market, and the pool of buyers—for a time—expanded sufficiently to keep the bandwagon rolling. But bubbles blown large enough inevitably pop. And then the old proverb is confirmed once again: "What the wise man does in the beginning, the fool does in the end."

Today the world's gold stock is about 170,000 metric tons. If all of this gold were melded together, it would form a cube of about 68 feet per side. (Picture it fitting comfortably within a baseball infield.) At $1,750 per ounce—gold's price as I write this—its value would be about $9.6 trillion. Call this cube pile "A."

Let's now create a pile "B" costing an equal amount. For that, we could buy all U.S. crop land (400 million acres with *output of about $200 billion annually), plus 16 Exxon Mobil's (the world's most profitable company, one earning more than $40 billion annually). After these purchases, we would have about $1 trillion left over for walking-around money (no sense feeling strapped after this buying binge). Can you imagine an investor with $9.6 trillion selecting pile "A" over pile "B"?*

To summarize Mr. Buffet's words in "my own speak," I would say that our primary focus should be on how to identify the greatest opportunities to increase the value of assets. [The best way to make sure that you have "food to eat" is to always be planting apple trees, not storing the seeds in barns and hoping that nothing happens to them.] You don't do this just by standing still, you have to roll up your sleeves, go to work, and look for those opportunities, like the men in the parable with 5 talents and 2 talents did.

What must we accept as our foundation before we can move forward? *One, increase is a part of our spiritual DNA. It is not only our mission, but it is our God-given mandate. Two, there is no place for fear, passivity, or laziness, among men and women of faith.*

We are a part of the The True Vine; we are being fed all of the nutrients that we need to be successful in bringing forth increase in every area of our lives, including our finances.

GROWING MORE SEED

The key to "growing seed" and "creating alternative streams of income" is for us to detach the "growth process" from our physical ability to make money.
– DEENA MARIE CARR

Volumes of books, articles, newsletters, and blogs have been written about the vast number of investment options available to U.S. investors, both at home and abroad. The NYSE Euronet, which operates the New York Stock Exchange (the largest stock exchange in the world based on market capitalization) offers over 8,000 listed issues, 1000 different derivative contracts, 2000 options issues.[1]

Aside from the stocks, bonds, mutual funds, ETFs (exchange traded funds), SPYDERS (SPDR-Standard & Poor's Depository Receipts) and other instruments available via the markets, there are many additional investments options such as annuities, real estate, precious metals, other commodities, hedge funds, etc.

The number of investment choices can be dizzying, if not completely confusing, which makes it so easy to delay putting a great amount of money and

1. Source: NYSE Euronet website, May, 2012

energy into something that you don't fully understand.

Goshen Principle #12:

The only way for us to "grow more seed" and create alternate streams of income is for us to detach the "growth process" from our physical ability to make money.

So how can we simplify the large and complex world of investing into something that is more manageable?

Personally, I take a different approach. I don't look at investing as a long list of investment instruments that are out there. For me, the simplest way to view the world of investing is by the graphic below.

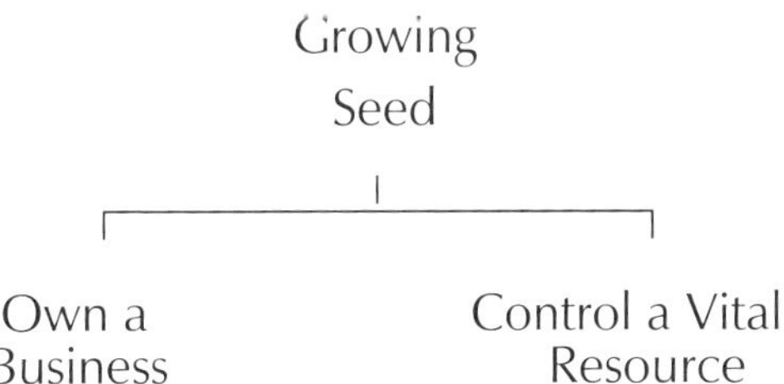

Goshen Simplification: The only way to "increase your seed" is to own a business or control a vital resource.

This means you need an entity that is able to generate value for you. Now there are two types of entities that create value for us: business entities (e.g., GE, Coca-Cola, your local dry cleaners, etc.) and vital resources (i.e., water, oil, etc.). Consequently, we can conclude that the only way to "increase your seed" is to own a business or control a vital resource.

Yes, this is a simplification, but in economics, there are numerous models, principles, and theories that are helpful, even though they are simplifications. In fact, some individuals have gone on to win the Nobel Prize in Economics based on these models.

And, more importantly, people have been able to extend these theories to solve more complex problems facing our world.

Growing Seed: Applying the Principle

As an example, let's take Lynne, a hairstylist in the Windy City.

She receives income by styling the hair of the various customers who come into the salon. Making money is a function of three things for Lynne: (1) the amount of time it takes her to complete a hairstyle *(speed),* (2) the number of hours she works in a day/week *(time),* and (3) the amount that she charges for services *(fees).*

If she wants to increase her income, she has to (1) work faster and process more customers,(2)work more hours, or (3)charge more money for her services.

Yes, in each case she is making more income, but in all instances the income is directly tied to how much she works personally.

Reminder: *Seed growing* means that you are making money independent of your effort alone. To do this, you must have an entity that perpetually creates value.

Let's go back to our hairstylist Lynne. If she wanted to apply Goshen principles, she would move from treating hair styling as a *job* to treating it as a *business.*

One way Lynn could do this is to create her own hair care product line or develop her own styling tools. She also could refine her technique and build the client-base to a point where she could hire other stylists, who then really want to work for her not just because she was able to give them a job, but because she could teach them valuable hair styling techniques. This would then generate income for Lynn whether she is working or just observing the hairstylists.

Lynn then could write a book which would allow her to share her philosophy and perspective across the country (i.e., with the book, Lynne's teaching expands beyond her ability to physically teach). Lynne can now make money from her books even while she is sleeping or driving to the salon.

Growing Seed Exercise #1:

What are some other things you think Lynne could do to turn hairstyling into a business—a perpetual income stream independent from the number of hours that she worked? Write them down and see how many you can come up with.

Growing Seed Exercise #2:

Are there any things you thought of for Lynne that you could apply to yourself? Are there any ideas that could help someone else you know? (Sometimes it is good to help others tap into their seed growing potential. In helping others, you may even be helping yourself tap into your own potential.)

ONE MORE EXAMPLE

Vance also lived in the Windy City, but a few years ago, he just had one too many sub-zero February days! Chicago is an amazing city in the summer, but occasionally the winters can really get to you. Sometimes, they are just a little too long, a little too cold and much too windy!

Vance decided he would move his family to Colorado to take advantage of a new job opportunity. Having lived in the city's South Loop area (i.e., just south of downtown Chicago) for such a long time, Vance decided to take advantage of the beautiful Colorado landscape, and buy some rural land northwest of Denver.

Vance's job allowed him to work anywhere he wanted, because much of his time was spent virtually traveling between their locations in Colorado and Salt Lake City, Utah.

After eight months in Colorado, he received a notice that geologists had discovered two resources on his property. The first was related to an oil well that he was originally told was inactive. It turns out that while there was no oil, they did find natural gas nearby.

The second piece of amazing news was that on another corner of his land, they found an artesian well which could produce natural spring water.

Vance loved his work, but was really excited to find this new source of wealth. Now he could work because he enjoyed it, not because he needed the money.

The developers wanted Vance to sell the land, but he decided that he was going to investigate other options where he could retain ownership of the property and its resources, while granting access to the land for drilling. He hoped that he could even develop a private label water bottling company.

Vance called his friend Mark from college who was an oil and gas consultant for a major U.S. management consulting firm.

Reminder: *Owning a business or controlling a vital resource puts you in the best position to create perpetual value.*

Before you close the book and say, "These are all great ideas but highly impractical for me because I do not want to own my own business and it is doubtful that I am going to stumble into some type of modern day 'Beverly Hillbillies' discovery!"

Never fear, you don't have to.

The previous graphic allowed us to simplify the world of investing. Well, let's dig a little deeper with the **Owning A Business** portion.

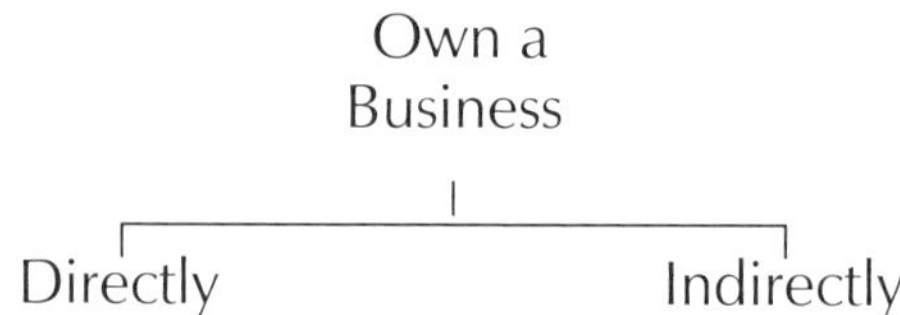

There are two ways to own a business. First, you can build a new company or acquire an existing enterprise, which you can own and run yourself; or you can be a limited partner while someone else manages the day-to-day operations.

This is what I refer to as **direct business ownership**—and are what our two examples have referenced.

Alternatively, you may feel you have no desire whatsoever to be involved in the risks and headaches of every day management. In this case, you can follow the second way to own a business, which is to have **indirect ownership** in that company. Such ownership is purchased via the financial markets.

A PIECE OF THE PIE

You may decide that you do not want to run a shoe business, but you believe that shoe companies are a really good idea, especially ones that make athletic shoes. In this case, you might choose a company like Nike, which is in the Fortune 500.

You say, "In addition to making quality shoes, they have a smart and productive approach to marketing. They do a really good job of signing high profile athletes, which seems to make kids willing to pay huge premiums over costs just to wear Nike shoes. And this is just in the USA. What if they begin to meet the unmet need for shoes around the world? Let me investigate them further."

Types of Business Ownership

Direct Ownership	Indirect Ownership
Create and run a business Buy an existing business Be a partner or limited partner in an existing business	Buy stock in the company Buy a mutual fund that holds that company's stock

We have applied this to business ownership, but the same is true for vital resources. In our example, Vance was the one who owned the natural resources.

You could also become an investment partner with Vance by funding a portion of the business expenses, for part ownership in the gas reserves and the artesian water well.

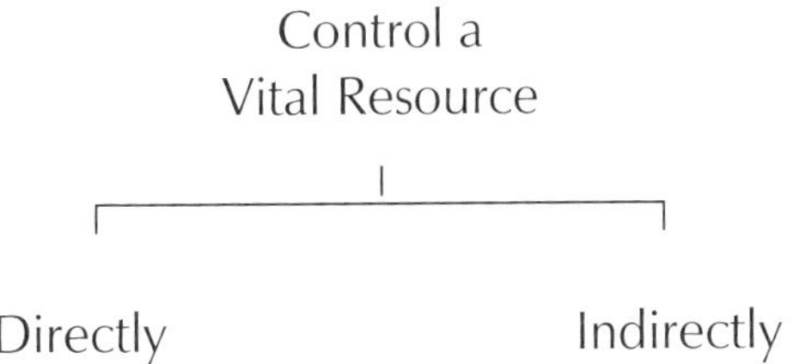

But this is not the only way to "own" a valuable resource. There are many companies in which you can purchase indirect ownership via the financial markets. This is one of the reasons why such markets exist. There are all types of companies and vital resources that you can purchase, from food to oil, platinum to real estate, and everything in between.

You can purchase the stock of these companies—or buy exchange traded funds or mutual funds that invest in these types of enterprises. The key is to first decide what it is that you want to do. Are you looking to own a business or are you looking to control a vital resource?

Growing Seed: Act like an owner

Many years ago, I was an intern at an asset management firm in Chicago. It was led by Gary Brinson, who is considered a pioneer in asset allocation and, according to CFA Magazine, one of investing's living legends. I worked in Domestic Equity for the Director of U.S. Research. There were many aspects that I found absolutely fascinating about the job—from studying things such as "alpha" and "hypergeometric distributions" to the meetings where analysts gave their insights regarding the companies in the portfolios. But near the top of the list was sitting with the analysts when they would call companies to interview the leadership or to schedule a meeting with the executives to gain more insight about the company.

They would begin the conversation with something like, "I am ___ from ____. We **own** your company" or "we own X percent of your company."

Initially, I was surprised by their language because

I thought they were just analysts and money managers, but quickly learned they were much more. They were shareholders—owners. And the other interesting point was that the corporations never treated them any differently. Their calls were immediately transferred to whomever they needed to speak to.

Over the years, I have met many people who have investments in companies via stock, mutual funds, or some other vehicle, and it is rather surprising how little they know about what they own.

I don't say this because I am naïve or condescending. I understand investing is challenging and that knowledge about investing written in simple and understandable language is hard to come by. If not, I would not be writing this book.

The surprising part is that while there are some people who are really seeking to learn more and work harder to better control and manage their investments, there is still a significant number of individuals who are comfortable "not knowing or understanding." They have completely "outsourced" their financial management.

Please don't get me wrong, I am not against having investment professionals helping you to manage your money, but that is exactly what it is. They are simply *helping you*—because you are the owner.

At this moment, you may not be able to take the multi-million dollar positions of an institutional money manager, *but you are still an owner and you have to approach your investment the same way that you would approach buying the company directly.* You need to answer the same type of questions.

- Does the company have strong products? Do they have additional products in the pipeline?

- Does it have a leading market position?

- Does it have a strong leadership team? Are they managing the company well?

- Is the company efficient and profitable? Do they have a clear strategy to continue the vision?

When you put on your owner's hat, there are a lot of questions you can ask. Don't be afraid to ask them.

Growing Seed Exercise #3:

Make a list of questions that you would want answered if you were the owner of a company. Here are a few to get you started:

- How strong are their products? Does the company have a pipeline of future products?

- Is the company growing?

- How efficient and profitable is the company?

- How strong is the management team? Do they have a succession plan?

Never forget that the first step in investing—in growing seed—is realizing that you are the owner of the business or the vital resource. You must act like and be engaged as an owner. As we said in chapter 4, *You must be diligent to know the state of your flocks, and attend to your herds; For riches are not forever, Nor does a crown endure to all generations.* The current global financial system is far more dynamic and rapidly moving than ever before. And this is not going to stop as man's knowledge increases (as Daniel prophesied in Daniel 12:4).

We can no longer afford to merely invest without an understanding of what we are investing in and why. Yes, you may employ *dollar cost averaging* and *asset allocation strategies* to lower your risk in the long run, but this does not mean you can simply bury your head in the sand and, as the expression goes, "mail it in."

The Lord has called us to excellence. Remember, *increase is a part of our spiritual DNA. It is not only our mission, but it is our God-given mandate.*

Chapter 7

Escaping the Debt Trap

This brings us to our fourth seed process of the GoWeM Framework—Leveraging Seed.

Leverage is a term that is used to describe the use of debt to finance the acquisition of assets. While we will focus on the use of debt, financial leverage can refer to other financial instruments that allow an investor to borrow money to acquire assets.

So the question is, why would the farmer use leverage? Well, before we answer that question, let's reflect on the proper use of debt.

In FATYF's classes on debt management, we discuss how debt should be used. First and foremost, debt should only be used to acquire assets. Why? Because with debt, you are not only going to have to pay back the amount of money that you borrowed, but you also have to make some type of interest payment as well.

If you are going to pay back more than the amount that you borrowed in the first place, then the "thing" that you borrowed has to increase in value and/or produce an income to cover both repayment of principle and the additional interest.

Failing to consider this is how a number of people get over their heads in debt, especially young college students. They are offered credit cards and, in an attempt to "build up their credit," they begin to use these cards to finance their lifestyle purchases—purchases far and above what they can pay when the monthly statement arrives.

Then, instead of paying the outstanding bill, they pay the minimum balance telling themselves that they will pay it off when they get out of college and "get a good paying job."

Others use their student loans in a similar manner. Yes, they borrow money to pay for tuition and other related expenses, but then they borrow well beyond what they need for school to once again pay for lifestyle purchases (e.g., clothing, electronic gadgets, trips, etc.). Again, assuming that they will take care of everything once they graduate and find a job.

We could spend more time and space discussing the many ways that people have stumbled in the use of debt, something that has mushroomed even more dramatically during the recent global financial crisis. However, we will save that for another time. Instead, let's focus on how the Goshen Wealth Management Framework carefully uses leverage for growth and management of ownership positions.

Leveraging Seed—Using Debt to "Expand the Farm"

Returning to our farmer's example, through the "seed process" we have been reviewing how the farmer acquires, manages and grows seed. Let's assume that through her initial acquisition of seed, she has all she needs to work at least the first phase of her farm. However, this is not always the case. Sometimes, one may need to borrow initially to get started.

In the case of the farmer, she may need to borrow "seed" so that she is able to plant the first crop. This means that after planting and then harvesting the crop, the farmer takes part of the harvest and pays back the bank or whomever she borrowed the seed from.

She takes a second part of the harvest and prepares to plant for next year's crop. Then she takes another portion and stores it in the grain silo. And finally, she takes some and sells it so that she can purchase other food and goods for the family. All of this began though with the acquisition of seed.

In this example, the farmer needed seed, but she could also be in a position where she needs to borrow not for the seeds, but for other things such as fertilizer, tools, irrigation, grain elevators, etc. In these instances, it makes sense to prudently borrow because this helps the farmer increase the productivity and make money.

Alternatively, we could have another situation where a farmer is borrowing from scratch. She needs to borrow money for the seed, equipment, fertilizer as well as the land. This clearly has more risk, but if the opportunity merits it and the farmer has a clear strategy for success, then once again it make sense to borrow. She may start out slow, but in a few years, with hard work and perseverance, she is going to have a prosperous business.

It is also quite realistic when we look at the growth of areas such as micro finance and micro lending in many developing countries. Pioneers like Nobel Laureate Dr. Muhummad Yunus found that they could make a tremendous impact on the economic conditions of families by lending to females so that they can engage in business.

These examples may appear to be a bit pedestrian, but they provide powerful lessons regarding how we should only use leverage to acquire or enhance assets. And in using leverage, we should carefully calculate the required investment, expected return, and corresponding risk associated with the venture.

A person who prudently uses leverage to stretch their initial capital can start out with very little and systematically grow it to have much.

SAM'S STORY

It was not very long ago that Wal-Mart was virtually unheard of except in certain parts of the U.S. Now it is basically a household name synonymous with wide selections of goods at extremely low prices. I know many people that love to shop at Wal-Mart and frequent their stores every week.

Wal-Mart is not only successful in the U.S., but it has expanded globally, making it one of the largest retailers in the world. Sounds great, doesn't it? But, it did not start out that way.

Sam Walton did not begin as a billionaire or even a millionaire for that matter. He was a franchisee with

Butler Brothers, which operated the Ben Franklin store chains. What is noteworthy is that one of the things that Sam Walton used to help get started with his franchise was a $20,000 loan from his father-in-law to purchase a store in Newport, Arkansas. In other words, Walton used leverage to help acquire seed.

Once he "had his farm up and running," he was able to pay back "the seed" to his father-in-law and continue to grow his business, step-by-step.

Leveraging Seed—Using Debt to "Retain Control"

We have talked about leverage being used to help acquire assets when you do not have quite enough capital. There are other reasons, however, why a person may choose to use debt. It can be a way of retaining ownership.

Going back to our example in chapter 6, Vance recently purchased land on which exploration geologists and geophysicists have found natural gas. The easy thing for Vance to do is to sell the land to the highest bidder and run to the bank. But, what if they give Vance a check for $5 million dollars, yet it turns out to be $300 million dollars of natural gas in the ground? Vance would have walked away from a lot of money. Now what if we turn the tables?

Let's say that Vance calls Mark, his close friend from college, who is an oil and gas consultant for a global management consulting firm. After talking through the entire situation, Mark and Vance decide to arrange a meeting with the geologists to better understand the details of what was found from their exploration. After the meeting, Mark and Vance are convinced that they have a real opportunity for significant wealth, but how do they tap into this resource?

They both have relevant business backgrounds, but they don't have the experience and the capital to drill wells and extract the natural gas—but Mark has an idea!

Mark went to business school with a young lady named Shana whose family owned and managed companies that acquire natural gas reserves for drilling and operating traditional shallow gas wells. With a good business plan, Mark felt that he could convince Shana and her family to invest in their project.

Mark and Vance came up with two options. The first was for Mark, Vance, and Shana to become equal partners in a new company that would be formed to extract the natural gas from the land.

The second option would be for Mark and Vance to retain 80% ownership of the company and sell Shana's family a 20% stake in the company, and sign a 20-year lease for the natural gas compression equipment critical to the extraction, gathering and transportation of the natural gas.

After several discussions, Mark and Vance decided to propose the second option. They really believed that there was a great deal of up-side in not only the amount of gas that could potentially be in the ground, but also in learning how to effectively run a small natural gas operation. Mark and Vance felt that they could parlay this opportunity into several others. They also believed they could always go back and sell their ownership stake if they later changed their minds.

What is the lesson here?

Vance and Mark are deciding to use leverage, which in this case is the long-term lease on the natural gas equipment, to avoid giving up more ownership of the company than they desire at this particular time.

Goshen Principle #13: One of the uses of debt is to retain ownership of an asset that one believes has significant value. Thus, leverage (debt) is a tool for deal making.

This is one of the reasons why a husband and wife may choose to use a mortgage to pay for their home. They want to retain complete ownership, and avoid a situation where someone else decides to move into the house with them because they are "co-owners."

On the other hand, four fraternity brothers might choose to pool their cash together to buy a small multi-unit building. In this instance, ownership is shared. This may make sense for four bachelors who are still working to establish themselves in their careers.

Leveraging Seed Exercise #1:

In chapter 6, we discussed how to grow seed through either the ownership of a business or control of a vital resource. You may have business ideas or ideas for inventions that you would love to act on. Let's work on those right here.

- List the business ideas that you have.
- List the ideas for inventions that you have?
- How much money would it take to act on each of your ideas?

Divide the ideas into three categories.

- Businesses or ideas that you would be willing to sell all or part of.
- Businesses or ideas that you would need to use debt to get started.
- Businesses or ideas that you would use debt to retain ownership.

Leveraging Seed Exercise #2:

Take two of your top ideas from the list and develop business plans to bring those businesses or ideas to market.

- Determine how much capital is required.
- If necessary, develop options for the amount of capital you would get for an ownership stake versus the amount that you need to borrow.

CHAPTER 8

A FINAL WORD

Together we have now walked through the entire Goshen Wealth Management framework:

- **Spiritual Context** – wealth has been created by God, and we tap into this wealth through our obedience to Him and diligence to His word.

- **Economic Context** – as we look to develop wealth, we must understand the economic environment in which we are operating. We should always adjust our strategy to ensure that it is the most effective, given the current and future economic conditions.

This takes us to the four Seed Processes, which are in the inner portion of the framework.

- **Gathering Seed:**
  Yes, we want to choose a way of generating an income based on the type of skills/occupations that are economically viable given current and future

conditions, but the most important way to generate an income or "gather seed" is to understand what God has called us to do in this season of our lives. Recognizing this allows us to maximize His ministry work through us, and thus maximize our income.

- Managing Seed:

    To consistently budget and manage our "seed," we must have a financial structure that enables us to use our finances to build both spiritually and naturally. By developing *Target Structures*, we can move our financial position to one that maximizes our ability to simultaneously make investments in the Kingdom of God and growth opportunities on earth.

- Growing Seed:

    To effectively increase our wealth, we must make money independent from the amount of effort that we can exert on our own. Instead, we must have entities that perpetually create value. The two main ways to do this is through owning businesses or controlling vital resources.

- Leveraging Seed:

    The ideal would be to do everything debt free. But sometimes there is an opportunity to acquire an asset (which is the only reason why we would use debt) that is temporarily beyond our immediate means. We can use "leverage" to help acquire that seed if we have a clear plan regarding the required investment, projected return, and potential risk. We may also choose to use leverage as a way of retaining control of an asset which has a great deal of future potential, and one for which we know we have the requisite knowledge and skills to cultivate that potential.

In our four Seed Processes, we want to target our time and energy on the first three: gathering, managing and growing. Ultimately, however, we want to focus on just two: growing and managing.

THIS WORLD IS NOT OUR HOME

Why all this attention and work on wealth and Bible-based financial management? What is this Goshen Wealth Management framework really about? Is it seeing how much we can acquire and how comfortably we can live while we are on earth? That's nice and probably our birthright as children of the Most High God, but it's not the most critical thing—and it is certainly not our focus.

Recently, I heard former Secretary of State, Dr. Condoleeza Rice, speak. She is truly a gifted and talented woman who has traveled the globe and served our nation well.

During her speech, she highlighted three shocks that, in her opinion, have forever changed our view of the world: September 11th 2001, the global financial crisis, and the Arab Spring. I would have to agree.

All of these things have changed our outlook regarding security, economic security and, I would say, the overall international political stability.

But when I look at the world through the lens of Bible eschatology, what is clear is that we are in the last days; and, as Hebrews 12:26–29 tells us, everything that can be shaken, is being shaken:

> *"...whose voice then shook the earth; but now He has promised, saying, 'Yet once more I shake not only the earth, but also heaven.' Now this, 'Yet once more,' indicates the removal of those things that are being shaken, as of things that are made, that the things which cannot be shaken may remain.*
>
> *Therefore, since we are receiving a kingdom which cannot be shaken, let us have grace, by which we may serve God acceptably with reverence and godly fear. For our God is a consuming fire."*

What does this means for us? It tells us:

- Now is the time for us to "be about our Father's business."

- Now is the time for us to "occupy until He comes."
- Now is the time for us to be "the head and not the tail."

We cannot sit back, close our eyes, cross our fingers, and wait for things to get better.The shaking has begun and, while it may pause, it is not going to ultimately stop. Like birth pains, as the time unfolds, the contractions will become more frequent and intense.

The hour has arrived for us to get our financial house in order. Not that we are going to place any confidence in the wealth of mammon. No, what we are doing is closing any doors which the enemy would use to exploit us, our families, our communities, and our nation. It is more important now than ever before, especially as I look at our global economic system.

This is not the time for the church to be divided based on partisan politics. I personally believe the church would be better served by leaving politics to the politicians and come together in prayer, revival and unity, from north to the south, east and the west.

The world needs a church that is acting as one body—The Body of Christ. We are the ones who need to be picking up the pace and building businesses and investing in resources that can serve to employ and help people in times of tremendous need —businesses and resources that can act as "arks of safety" in times of uncertainty or great distress. (Remember, *"...as it was in the days of Noah..."* but Noah had built an ark.)

Our faith does not constrict in days like these, but it expands, because we know that "our redemption draws nigh."

Use the Goshen Wealth Management Framework to position yourself and your family for long-term, Godly success in everything you do. And just as God not only preserved but prospered His children in seasons of plenty and famine while they were in Egypt, He will do the same for His children now. But we must be rooted and grounded in Him in every area of our lives, including our finances.

For a Complete List of Media
Resources or to Schedule the Author
For Speaking Engagements, Contact:

Deena Marie Carr
Finance: According to Your Faith
C/o Christian Heritage Training Center
160 Marquette Road
Chicago, IL 60637

Phone: 877-328-9375 Internet: www.fatyf.org
Email: info@financeaccordingtoyourfaith.org